**Richard Harris & Christoper**

# Build**Up**
## Reading Level **1**

Richard Harris & Christoper



Cover/Interior Design: Design YoungZoo

ISBN: 978-89-90545-67-1

**Desk Copy Request / Information**
To place your desk copy request or for more information,
please contact the following office:
Tel: (02)3273-4300    Fax: (02)3273-4303
Homepage: www.wcbooks.co.kr

# Contents

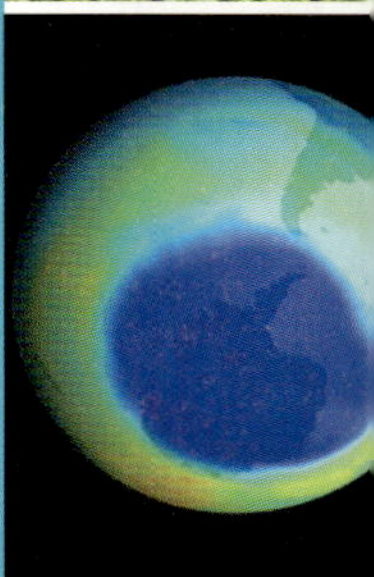

**Pre-reading activity**

1. Why do we sleep?
2. What is REM sleep?
3. How does sleeping help us?

 T1

1  Sleep is a natural requirement for everyone. From tired office workers to exhausted mothers, sleep signals to us all at the end of a hard day. It's nature's way of telling us that we need to **recharge** our batteries. Doctors advise us to get a good eight hours' sleep, but how much is enough? Well, scientists have been trying to answer this question for years. Yet the surprising fact is no one knows exactly why or how we sleep and how many hours are ideal. It's still sort of a mystery.

2  Until the early 1950s, many scientists believed the body and brain rested during sleep. Then one day a curious scientist decided to study people's sleep habits. He discovered that sometimes the sleepers' eyes made **rapid** movements. It looked like they were watching "something" with their eyes closed. The eye movements lasted between 5 and 30 minutes. He called these **periods** REM sleep, for Rapid Eye Movement.

3  Curious about what was happening to these people during REM sleep, the scientist decided to wake some of them up during their REM periods. What he discovered was interesting. They were in the midst of having **vivid** dreams. Further studies showed that sleepers' heart rates rose quickly during REM sleep. Their breathing, heartbeat, and blood going to the brain also increased. Instead of being a time of rest, REM sleep seemed to be a time when the body is very **active**.

4  To this day, scientists still don't know why there is brain activity during sleep. But some research has suggested that if a person gets more REM sleep, it makes learning easier. Some believe that it is crucial to brain development because babies spend a lot of time in REM sleep. However, one thing all the scientists agree on is that sleep is necessary. Without it, people can't function properly. So make sure to have a good night's sleep every night!

## Vocabulary Study

**A  Choose and write the correct word.**

| active | period | recharge | vivid | rapid |
| --- | --- | --- | --- | --- |

1.  The butterfly makes ____________ movements with its wings.

2.  You have to be ____________ to be healthy and fit.

3.  Batteries that you can ____________ are good for the earth.

4.  The artist used ____________ colors in his paintings.

5.  People must have ____________s of rest during the day.

**B  Replace the underlined words with a synonym from the box.**

| surprising | mystery | rapid | necessary | vivid |
| --- | --- | --- | --- | --- |

1.  The news of his accident was <u>startling</u>.

2.  Many children have <u>colorful</u> imaginations.

3.  Most people enjoy solving a <u>puzzle</u>.

4.  Doctors believe a good diet is <u>essential</u>.

5.  The dancer made <u>swift</u> movements with his feet.

## Main idea

This story is about ____________.

a. scientists                    b. the brain

c. REM sleep                    d. eyes

## Paragraph Understanding

Choose the correct answer.

1. Paragraph ____    Scientists say that sleep is important for everyone.
2. Paragraph ____    Research was conducted in the 1950s.
3. Paragraph ____    The body is not resting during REM sleep.
4. Paragraph ____    Sleepers have periods of rapid eye movements.

## Looking for detail

Circle the correct answer.

1. Scientists thought the brain rested during sleep until the early ________.
   - a. 1950s
   - b. 1960s
   - c. 1850s
   - d. 1940s

2. REM stands for ____________.
   - a. recharge everyone's mind
   - b. really excellent movements
   - c. rapid eye movements
   - d. rapid early movies

3. Which paragraph talks about what happens during REM sleep?
   - a. Paragraph 1
   - b. Paragraph 2
   - c. Paragraph 3
   - d. Paragraph 4

4. No one denies the fact that sleep is ____________.
   - a. useless
   - b. needed
   - c. irregular
   - d. dispensable

## Developing Skills

**Rearrange the words below to make correct sentences.**

1. body   is   the   active   during   very   sleep   REM

   _______________________________________________

2. woke   during   people   he   up   REM   their   periods

   _______________________________________________

3. is   sleeping   a   mystery   still

   _______________________________________________

4. have   vivid   people   dreams   night   at

   _______________________________________________

5. heartbeat   increase   people's   breathing   and

   _______________________________________________

## T2 Summary & Listening Practice

**Read the paragraph and fill in as many blanks as you can.
Then listen to the recording and fill in the rest of the blanks.**

Sleeping is still a ① _____________ . Originally, many scientists had thought the brain '② _____________' when people slept. Then a scientist discovered people went through REM sleep. This proved that the body is very ③ _____________ during sleep. Whether dreaming or just tossing and turning in bed, people's breathing, heartbeat, and blood to the brain ④ _____________ . Many mysteries remain about why we sleep, but scientists all agree that it is ⑤ _____________ .

**Pre-reading activity**

1. Where do we get new words?
2. Do you know where the word *sandwich* comes from?
3. Are there any Italian words in English?

 T3

1   Have you ever wondered where words come from? Language is very fluid, especially English. New words can come from almost anywhere — even from an American President! That's right! One of the most common childhood toys, the "teddy bear," was named after President Theodore Roosevelt. Theodore Roosevelt was affectionately known as "Teddy" and after saving a small bear from being shot, he **gained** a new nickname. Soon after, when the story of the bear incident circulated, toymakers began making **stuffed** toy bears. The new toy was called the teddy bear, of course.

2   Other times, things are sometimes named for the people who discovered or invented them. The word *sandwich* comes from the British Earl of Sandwich. He came up with the idea of putting food between two slices of bread. Likewise, the watt, a measurement of electricity, was named after the inventor, James Watt. Anders Dahl had a flower named after him, the dahlia. **Countless** words were created this way.

3   Many words are **simply** borrowed from other languages. For instance, the words *pizza* and *cappuccino* are Italian. *Banjo* is African; *rodeo* is Spanish, and so on. On the other hand, compound words like *website* and *desktop* have been **formed** by putting existing words together. Sometimes words are created by taking a mechanical sound and giving it meaning, like *whoosh* and *vroom*.

4   With over one million words in the English language, it is surprisingly flexible with thousands more words are added each year. But without meaning, words are useless. That's why our language is always changing and growing, influenced by everything from pop culture to music and art and food. It all affects the way we use words in context.

## Vocabulary Study

**A  Choose and write the correct word.**

| stuffed | gained | simply | formed | countless |

1. ___________ follow the directions on the box.

2. I can make a ___________ doll.

3. He used a napkin and ___________ a swan-like shape with it.

4. There are ___________ insects that haven't been discovered yet.

5. We ___________ invaluable experience during that summer.

**B  Replace the underlined words with a synonym from the box.**

| countless | inventor | fluid | affectionately | circulated |

1. In many ways, the Internet is very flexible.

2. The children were tenderly cared for by the kind nurse.

3. His fame spread across the country.

4. Numerous people go picnicking at the park.

5. Thomas Edison was a great creator.

## Main idea

This story is about ______________.

a. the making of new words      b. new ideas and inventions

c. the making of new names      d. new languages and cultures

## Paragraph Understanding

**Choose the correct answer.**

1. Paragraph ___    Things can be named for the people who invented them.
2. Paragraph ___    The English language is always growing.
3. Paragraph ___    New words can be borrowed or put together.
4. Paragraph ___    The teddy bear was named after a famous U.S. President.

## Looking for detail

**Circle the correct answer.**

1. The word *rodeo* comes from ___________.
   - a. Italy
   - b. America
   - c. Spain
   - d. Africa

2. The watt is a measurement of ___________.
   - a. electricity
   - b. time
   - c. distance
   - d. speed

3. Which paragraph talks about fitting a sound to a meaning?
   - a. Paragraph 1
   - b. Paragraph 2
   - c. Paragraph 3
   - d. Paragraph 4

4. Dictionaries must be ___________.
   - a. very unhelpful
   - b. changed often
   - c. revised every day
   - d. translated into English

## Developing Skills

**Rearrange the words below to make correct sentences.**

1. started   make   to   toymakers   bears   stuffed

   _______________________________________________

2. was   Anders   Dahl   after   the   named   dahlia

   _______________________________________________

3. formed   together   two   by   putting   website   old   was   words

   _______________________________________________

4. year   are   of   words   thousands   new   made   every

   _______________________________________________

5. its   sounds   whoosh   meaning   like

   _______________________________________________

### T4   Summary & Listening Practice

**Read the paragraph and fill in as many blanks as you can.**
**Then listen to the recording and fill in the rest of the blanks.**

New words are ① ___________ coming from many sources, making English a highly ② ___________ language. Words are sometimes named after people who discovered or invented things. Many words are ③ ___________ from other languages like Italian, Spanish or African ④ ___________. Other words are made by putting two words together. Still other words are made up by giving meaning to a ⑤ ___________ sound. The English language keeps growing as the world keeps changing.

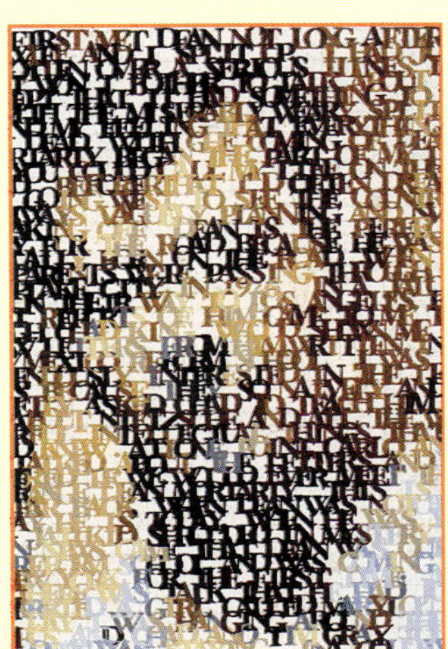

 T5

1. The violinist Midori started playing at the young age of three. She was a very gifted player but had little experience in front of audiences. So, in July 1986, as a 14-year-old girl, Midori was invited to an important summer music festival to perform as a **soloist**. Although talented as a soloist, she needed to **demonstrate** that she could perform for an audience. It would be a test under pressure.

2. Midori's solo piece was going well until the last moment when a string on Midori's violin snapped! The audience gasped. But Midori reacted with grace under pressure. Very calmly, Midori borrowed an instrument from another violinist, something many experienced musicians might not have done so **effortlessly**. Then she started to play again as if nothing had happened.

3. However, this was Midori's unlucky night. Only minutes later, the same thing happened again. Another string snapped! Yet Midori remained calm. She just borrowed a second violin and continued on. Nothing seemed to bother her as she finished her solo piece successfully. When she finished, the audience, the orchestra, and the conductor cheered and **applauded**.

4. Midori's solo performance made the front pages of the local newspapers. People seemed surprised that such a young girl could have so much poise under difficult circumstances. She became even more famous. But she didn't understand the **fuss**. The reason she kept on playing was simple. She said, "I didn't want to stop. I love that piece."

## Vocabulary Study

**A  Choose and write the correct word.**

> demonstrate    soloist    effortlessly    applauded    fuss

1. Chris can draw great pictures ___________.

2. The audience ___________ after the performance.

3. My mom made a ___________ when I got an A on my test.

4. Anna needs to ___________ her ability as a producer.

5. You need to be talented to be a ___________.

**B  Replace the underlined words with a synonym from the box.**

> started    gifted    calmly    experienced    poise

1. She has a lot of grace when speaking in public.

2. Yo Yo Ma is a talented musician.

3. William Zinsser is a skilled writer.

4. Let's solve this problem peacefully.

5. The sisters launched their own business.

## Main idea

This story is about _____________.

    a. being a great player
    b. being calm under pressure
    c. making many mistakes
    d. loving music

## 03

## Paragraph Understanding

Choose the correct answer.

1. Paragraph ___   A string snapped on Midori's violin.
2. Paragraph ___   Her story was in the newspaper and Midori became famous.
3. Paragraph ___   Midori was invited to be a soloist at a music festival.
4. Paragraph ___   Another string snapped, but Midori kept playing.

## Looking for detail

Circle the correct answer.

1. Midori's violin string snapped ___________.
   a. once
   b. twice
   c. three times
   d. never

2. Everyone ___________ Midori's playing and poise.
   a. cheered
   b. hated
   c. disliked
   d. laughed at

3. Which paragraph talks about being a good soloist?
   a. Paragraph 1
   b. Paragraph 2
   c. Paragraph 3
   d. Paragraph 4

4. After Midori's solo performance, she probably ___________.
   a. never performed again
   b. kept on having bad luck
   c. learned a different instrument
   d. had more solo performances

## Developing Skills

**Rearrange the words below to make correct sentences.**

1. started   three   Midori   playing   violin   the   at

_________________________________________________

2. sighed   the   in   audience   relief

_________________________________________________

3. she   a   on   just   second   and   violin   borrowed   went

_________________________________________________

4. were   at   people   Midori's   surprised   poise

_________________________________________________

5. playing   didn't   to   want   stop   Midori

_________________________________________________

### T6    Summary & Listening Practice

**Read the paragraph and fill in as many blanks as you can.**
**Then listen to the recording and fill in the rest of the blanks.**

At the age of 14, Midori was invited to a music festival as a ① _____________ . While playing, a string on her violin ② _____________ not once, but twice. But Midori remained calm and borrowed a violin from another violinist. Everyone ③ _____________ Midori's ④ _____________ . Her ⑤ _____________ made the front pages of the local newspapers. As a result, she became more famous.

# 04 chew, chew, chewing gum

 T7

1. Chew it, blow it, stretch it, and snap it. For many, chewing gum is a regular habit. And check out those **flavors**. Spearmint, peppermint, cinnamon, coffee, grape, and strawberry! Whoa~ that's a lot of different choices and that's just the start. Today, gum is found everywhere, in convenience stores, supermarkets, gas stations, and airport shops. We can chew as much as we want. Those who chew it think there is nothing better. But there are others who think it is a **disgusting** and dirty habit. What do you think?

2. So, where did chewing gum come from? Well, chewing gum dates back over a thousand years to the Mayas, who lived in Central America. They were a brilliant people who invented many things that we take for granted today. These include mathematical systems, a writing system, and ... chewing gum!

3. Around the Mayan cities, the sapodilla tree grew in the rain forests. The Mayas prized the tree for its delicious fruit and for its strong red wood. But more amazing was a sticky white **fluid** inside the bark of the tree. The fluid would harden into a gummy **material**. Although not that tasty, it was nice to chew. The material was called chicle and it is the main ingredient used in chewing gum today.

4. Hundreds of years later, this chicle was exported when European travelers transported it to other countries. But one thing was lacking — a pleasant taste. In the 1860s, an **inventor** in the United States had the wonderful idea of adding a sweet artificial flavor to it. He thought that chicle would be more popular if it had a better taste. That's the beginning of the modern chewing gum industry.

## Vocabulary Study

**A  Choose and write the correct word.**

> flavors    disgusting    fluid    material    inventor

1.  You need to drink lots of ___________s when you have a cold.

2.  Picking one's nose is a ___________ habit.

3.  There are so many ___________ of ice cream.

4.  Steel is a very strong ___________.

5.  Alexander Graham Bell was a famous ___________.

**B  Replace the underlined words with a synonym from the box.**

> choice    brilliant    yummy    later    wonderful

1.  The view is <u>terrific</u> at the top of the mountain.

2.  Many say Einstein was a <u>smart</u> man.

3.  You have an <u>option</u> of tea or coffee.

4.  The whole dinner was <u>delicious</u>.

5.  Many years <u>after</u>, the park was gone.

## Main idea

This story is about ______________.
    a.  the sapodilla tree        b.  who the Mayas were
    c.  different kinds of bubble gum    d.  who made the first chewing gum

## Paragraph Understanding

**Choose the correct answer.**

1. Paragraph ____    The Mayas found chicle in the bark of a tree.
2. Paragraph ____    Today there are many different kinds of gum.
3. Paragraph ____    A sweet flavor was added to chicle.
4. Paragraph ____    The Mayas invented chewing gum.

## Looking for detail

**Circle the correct answer.**

1. The Mayas had a ____________.
   - a. math system
   - b. a gum factory
   - c. a tree farm
   - d. chicle plant

2. The sapodilla tree grew ____________.
   - a. in the rain forests
   - b. all year round
   - c. everywhere in the U.S.
   - d. fast

3. Which paragraph talks about an American inventor?
   - a. Paragraph 1
   - b. Paragraph 2
   - c. Paragraph 3
   - d. Paragraph 4

4. Chewing gum probably wouldn't have been popular if ____________.
   - a. there had been no travelers
   - b. flavor had not been added to it
   - c. chicle had not reached Asia
   - d. the Mayas were living now

## Developing Skills

**Rearrange the words below to make correct sentences.**

1. Central    lived    the    Mayas    America    in

   _______________________________________________

2. chew    the    was    to    nice    chicle

   _______________________________________________

3. United States    an    in    the    had    good    inventor    idea    a

   _______________________________________________

4. red    the    had    tree    yummy    and    strong    wood    fruit

   _______________________________________________

5. other    travelers    the    to    countries    took    chicle

   _______________________________________________

---

T8    **Summary & Listening Practice**

**Read the paragraph and fill in as many blanks as you can.**
**Then listen to the recording and fill in the rest of the blanks.**

Chewing gum was first used over a thousand years ago by the Mayas. They had discovered a white ① _____________ in the bark of the sapodilla tree. Inside the tree was a fluid that ② _____________ into a gummy material. The Mayas called it chicle and it's the main ③ _____________ used in making chewing gum today. In the 1860s, an American inventor added a sweet ④ _____________ to the chicle to make it more popular. Hence, the modern chewing gum ⑤ _____________ was born.

# THE YELLOW KID

T9

1 At the end of the 19th century, a young **aspiring** publisher, Joseph Pulitzer, was searching for new ways to make money. He was the publisher of the New York World and other daily newspapers in the U.S. In 1895, Pulitzer asked Richard Outcault, one of his **artists**, to start drawing a weekly **cartoon**. It was printed in the Sunday edition of the World. Pulitzer hoped it would liven up his newspaper and increase sales.

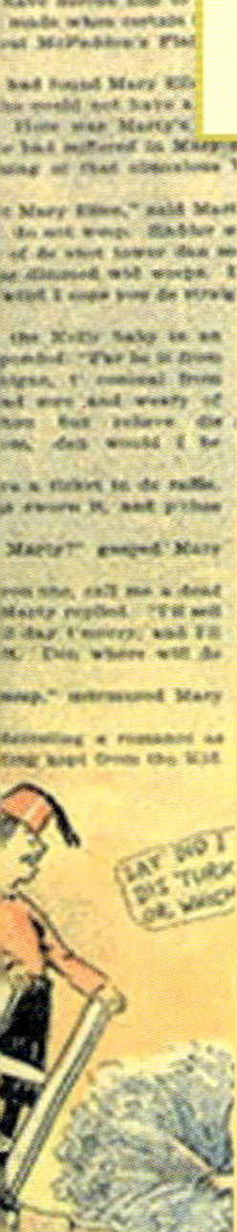

2 The new cartoon was called "Down Hogan's Alley" and Outcault chose a funny little boy as his main character. The boy was very peculiar, being bald and having ears that stuck out to the sides. He was always barefoot and dressed in a nightshirt. To tell the cartoon story, the words spoken by the character were written on his clothes. Although the boy had no name, Pulitzer began using colored printing inks. The boy's nightshirt was printed yellow. So, people called him "The Yellow Kid."

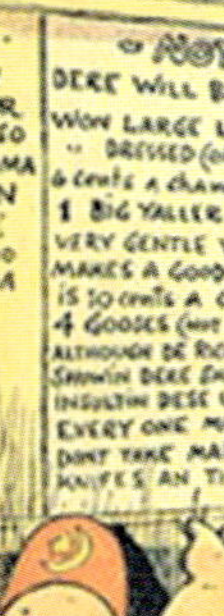

3 The cartoon was an instant hit. So Outcault asked his **boss** for a raise, but Pulitzer refused. Eventually, Outcault quit and went to work for another newspaper, the *Journal American*. Even though Pulitzer hired another cartoonist to draw "The Yellow Kid," Outcault kept drawing the same cartoon for his new newspaper. So, the cartoon was appearing in both papers.

4 Other cartoons followed and with them, new styles of telling stories. "The Katzenjammer Kids" cartoon came out in 1897. The German American artist Rudolph Dirks created a **strip**, or series of cartoons, to tell a short story. Each successive cartoon "box" told a new part of the story. He wrote the characters' words in "balloons" above their heads. By 1910, hundreds of "comic strips" were appearing in newspapers across America. But "The Yellow Kid" is still considered the first modern newspaper comic.

## Vocabulary Study

**A** Choose and write the correct word.

> aspiring    cartoon    boss    strip    artists

1. The ___________ painted pictures of a garden.

2. Kids like reading and watching ___________ s.

3. Mary was an ___________ singer.

4. His ___________ yelled at him for being late.

5. My favorite comic ___________ is Garfield.

**B** Replace the underlined words with a synonym from the box.

> popular    funny    bald    a hit    modern

1. The singer Seven is very well-liked.

2. The style of the building is new and current.

3. Her grandfather is hairless.

4. I like sitcoms that are humorous.

5. The groups new CD was successful.

## Main idea

This story is about ______________.

    a. the first newspaper      b. how to be a cartoonist

    c. the first newspaper comic      d. how to be a good publisher

## Paragraph Understanding

### Choose the correct answer.

1. Paragraph ___  Outcault drew "The Yellow Kid" for another newspaper.
2. Paragraph ___  The boy was called "The Yellow Kid" because of his nightshirt.
3. Paragraph ___  Pulitzer started a weekly cartoon.
4. Paragraph ___  The comic strip was created.

## Looking for detail

### Circle the correct answer.

1. Joseph Pulitzer ran a newspaper in ___________.
   a. Chicago
   b. New York
   c. Hogan
   d. L.A.

2. "The Yellow Kid" had words written on ___________.
   a. his clothes
   b. his head
   c. his barefoot
   d  his ears

3. Which paragraph talks about writing word balloons above characters' heads?
   a. Paragraph 1
   b. Paragraph 2
   c. Paragraph 3
   d. Paragraph 4

4. Comic strips ___________.
   a. help sell newspapers
   b. must be in color
   c. make artists poor
   d. need a monster character

## Developing Skills

**Rearrange the words below to make correct sentences.**

1. Sunday   came   the   edition   the   out   cartoon   on

   _______________________________________________

2. bald   barefoot   and   character   the   was   main

   _______________________________________________

3. but   refused   artist   the   his   a   raise   boss   wanted

   _______________________________________________

4. cartoons   Rudolph Dirks   a   of   created   strip

   _______________________________________________

5. for   went   Outcault   to   another   work   newspaper

   _______________________________________________

### T 10   Summary & Listening Practice

**Read the paragraph and fill in as many blanks as you can.**
**Then listen to the recording and fill in the rest of the blanks.**

In 1895, Joseph Pulitzer had Outcault start ① ___________
a weekly cartoon. The cartoon was called "Down Hogan's
Alley." The main ② ___________ was a funny little boy,
dressed in a nightshirt with big ears. The nightshirt was
③ ___________ in yellow, so people started calling him
"The Yellow Kid." Then the artist, Rudolph Dirks, created
a ④ ___________ of cartoons — a new ⑤ ___________ for
that time. By 1910, comic strips became popular, but "The
Yellow Kid" was the first modern newspaper comic.

 T 11

1 Women have always struggled to be treated equally. Today, it is common practice in most countries to allow women the **right** to **vote**, but it wasn't always that way. When women first wanted the right to vote, men laughed at the idea. They thought that women belonged in the home, cooking and making babies. One U.S. President even said, "Sensible women do not want to vote." But this did not stop women from trying.

2 Women first began to organize for the right to vote in 1848. A meeting was organized in Seneca Falls, New York, to discuss the matter. At the meeting, some women declared it was their **duty** to vote. They believed they should be able to vote since they paid taxes just as men did. They wanted to have a say in how their government was run and wanted to have their voice heard.

3 For the next 70 years, women made speeches, wrote letters, and marched in streets. They were called "suffragettes" because they wanted **suffrage**, or the right to vote. As time went by, more and more men gradually agreed with the women. After all, it only seemed fair to let them vote too. Women in the territory of Wyoming (later to be a state), had voted since 1869. By the end of the century, many states had passed laws of their own to let women vote.

4 Finally, in 1919, the United States passed the Nineteenth Amendment to the Constitution. It gave all American women the right to vote. A year later, on a sunny Tuesday, women had their first chance to vote in a presidential election. It was November 1920, a long way from that meeting in 1848. Almost eight million women voters helped **elect** a new President. Now, women themselves are voted into office. Someday soon, a woman President is likely to be elected — maybe even in 2008.

## Vocabulary Study

**A** **Choose and write the correct word.**

| right | duty | suffrage | vote | elect |
|---|---|---|---|---|

1. The students have to ___________ a class president.

2. People have a ___________ to say what they want.

3. Who wants to have pizza for lunch? Let's ___________.

4. Mike's ___________ was to throw out the garbage.

5. ___________ is something that everyone wants.

**B** **Replace the underlined words with a synonym from the box.**

| certainly | sensible | declared | marched | likely |
|---|---|---|---|---|

1. The parade <u>walked</u> down the street.

2. Rain is <u>expected</u> to fall this afternoon.

3. He will <u>surely</u> win the Spelling Bee.

4. The principal <u>stated</u> that students must be on time.

5. My mother is a very <u>practical</u> and intelligent woman.

## Main idea

This story is about _____________.
   a. women in the government
   b. women and suffering
   c. women becoming president
   d. women's right to vote

## Paragraph Understanding

**Choose the correct answer.**

1. Paragraph ___     In 1920, women voted in their first presidential election.
2. Paragraph ___     Women had a meeting to declare their right to vote.
3. Paragraph ___     More men agreed with them, so many states let women vote.
4. Paragraph ___     People used to laugh at the idea of women voting.

## Looking for detail

**Circle the correct answer.**

1. Women in 1848 had to pay ___________.
   a.  tuition
   b.  taxes
   c.  men
   d.  the president

2. The Nineteenth Amendment let women ___________.
   a.  vote
   b.  march
   c.  work
   d.  speak

3. Which paragraph talks about Wyoming allowing women to vote?
   a.  Paragraph 1
   b.  Paragraph 2
   c.  Paragraph 3
   d.  Paragraph 4

4. Someday soon, the U.S. may ___________.
   a.  let children vote
   b.  take away taxes
   c.  use the Internet for voting
   d.  have a women President

## Developing Skills

**Rearrange the words below to make correct sentences.**

1. belonged   home   thought   people   women   at

_________________________________________________

2. government   voice   have   wanted   women   to   a   in

_________________________________________________

3. right   suffrage   the   is   vote   to

_________________________________________________

4. in   almost   million   women   election   the   eight   voted

_________________________________________________

5. vote   let   laws   states   many   passed   to   women

_________________________________________________

## T 12    Summary & Listening Practice

**Read the paragraph and fill in as many blanks as you can.**
**Then listen to the recording and fill in the rest of the blanks.**

Women weren't always allowed to vote. Women first began to ① _________ to gain the right to vote in 1848. They thought it was their ② _________ to vote. They wanted to have a ③ _________ in their own government. For 70 years, suffragettes made speeches, wrote letters, and ④ _________ in the streets. Slowly, more and more men started to agree with the women. In 1919, the U.S. ⑤ _________ all American women the right to vote.

1  Do you have a curious mind? Do you think of yourself as someone who is good at **solving** puzzles? Well, about 50 years ago, a scientist and writer named Thor Heyerdahl from Norway was so determined to figure out a mystery that he risked his life trying to do it. He traveled more than 4,300 miles to try and explain how **explorers** traveled across the ocean!

2  Hundreds of years ago, explorers found people living on the South Sea Islands of the Pacific Ocean. They discovered nice farms and villages. They also found great **temples** and tall stone statues. The explorers were naturally curious about these people. Where did they come from? How had they traveled to these tiny islands in the middle of the world's largest ocean?

3  Well, Thor Heyerdahl thought he knew the answer. Thor knew the Indians of Peru in South America had also built tall stone statues, temples, and large villages, just like in the South Sea Islands. He believed that hundreds of years ago these Indians had sailed to the South Sea Islands on small **rafts**. But many other famous scientists disagreed with him. They thought it was impossible to sail 4,300 miles just on a floating raft.

4  So, Thor decided to test his **theory**. He built a wooden raft just like the ones the Indians of Peru used. He called it the *Kon-Tiki*. Then on April 28, 1947, he and five friends set sail from Peru, out into the wild blue ocean. The voyage was very dangerous and they had no modern radio communication equipment. They sailed through extreme heat and huge waves, and even encountered killer sharks! Finally, after 101 days, they made it. They reached the South Sea Islands on their raft. Thor's daring voyage showed that he could have been right. The Indians of Peru could have sailed to those faraway islands. In this respect, Thor Heyerdahl can be thought of as a great explorer of the truth.

## Vocabulary Study

**A  Choose and write the correct word.**

| solve | explorers | temples | raft | theory |
|---|---|---|---|---|

1. Huckleberry Finn went down the river on ___________ .

2. This math problem is too hard. I can't ___________ it.

3. Joe saw many ___________ on his trip in Thailand.

4. ___________ are probably curious people.

5. Let's test your ___________ to see if it's possible.

**B  Replace the underlined words with a synonym from the box.**

| pretty | curious | huge | daring | faraway |
|---|---|---|---|---|

1. Stuntmen do <u>brave</u> stunts all the time.

2. Tahiti is <u>very</u> far from France.

3. Diana traveled to <u>distant</u> countries.

4. China is a <u>large</u> country.

5. They were <u>interested</u> to know about their new neighbor.

## Main idea

This story is about ______________ .

    a.  traveling the Pacific Ocean      b.  proving a theory

    c.  Peru Indians      d.  stone statues

## Paragraph Understanding

**Choose the correct answer.**

1. Paragraph ____    Thor and his men made it to the islands on a raft.
2. Paragraph ____    A scientist from Norway traveled far to solve a mystery.
3. Paragraph ____    Thor thought the Indians of Peru had sailed to the islands.
4. Paragraph ____    Explorers found people living on the South Sea Islands.

## Looking for detail

**Circle the correct answer.**

1. Thor thought the Indians of Peru had lived on the South Sea Islands because ___________.
   a. they had the same statues and temples
   b. they used the same rafts
   c. they spoke the same language
   d. they lived in small villages

2. Thor called his raft ___________.
   a. *Kona-Toto*    b. *Kon-Tiki*    c. *Norway*    d. *Peru*

3. Which paragraph talks about explorers finding farms and villages on the South Sea Islands?
   a. Paragraph 1                     b. Paragraph 2
   c. Paragraph 3                     d. Paragraph 4

4. Thor's voyage ___________.
   a. solved the mystery          b. showed that his theory was possible
   c. discredited his research    d. made other scientists disagree more

## Developing Skills

**Rearrange the words below to make correct sentences.**

1. mystery   wanted   explain   to   a   Thor

______________________________________________

2. explorers   villages   the   found   and   farms   nice

______________________________________________

3. impossible   many   was   scientists   theory   thought   Thor's

______________________________________________

4. hot   the   and   sharks   men   weather   killer   fought   the

______________________________________________

5. 101   they   it   made   days   after

______________________________________________

### T 14   Summary & Listening Practice

**Read the paragraph and fill in as many blanks as you can.**
**Then listen to the recording and fill in the rest of the blanks.**

Thor Heyerdahl was a scientist from Norway. He traveled far to explain a ① ___________ . A long time ago, explorers found farms, villages, temples, and tall stone ② ___________ on the South Sea Islands of the Pacific Ocean. This made them ③ ___________ as to who built them. Thor thought the Indians of Peru must have sailed there on rafts. Thor built a ④ ___________ raft and sailed the long voyage toward the islands. He made it after 101 days. He showed that his theory might be ⑤ ___________ .

# 08   Rita Levi-MONTALCINI'S DISCOVERY

 T 15

1  Rita Levi-Montalcini was a young Jewish woman growing up in Italy. She had a passion for science and wanted to study it, but her father wanted her to get married. After much discussion for two years, Rita was finally able to change her father's mind. In the end, he let her go to medical school to pursue her dreams. When she **graduated**, she found she couldn't get work as a scientist. At the time, Jewish people in Italy weren't allowed to work at many kinds of jobs.

2  However, nothing could stop Rita. She was so determined that she set up a **laboratory** in her bedroom and worked on her own. What really fascinated her was how cells grew. She did her research using simple household items such as eggs, an old **microscope**, and a sewing needle. She had no other tools. In her experiments with eggs, Rita discovered a chemical that makes nerve cells grow. It was a miracle she succeeded.

3  But a sudden change in world events threatened everything that Rita had worked for. World War II started and Rita and her family were in danger. The Nazis in Germany began killing Jewish people all over Europe. So Rita hid in a small apartment in Turin, Italy. For the entire war — four years — this **tiny** room was her entire life. When the war was finally over and Italy and Germany surrendered, Rita got a great offer. She was invited to work in America.

4  Rita continued her scientific work in America. Over the next 15 years, Rita discovered more growth **chemicals**. This led more scientists to follow her work. Soon, other discoveries were made. Today, theses chemicals are used for many things. Among them, they are used to grow new skin on people who have been badly burned. In 1986, Rita Levi-Montalcini won the Nobel Prize for her work in science.

## Vocabulary Study

**A  Choose and write the correct word.**

> graduated    laboratory    microscope    tiny    chemicals

1.  The students went into the ____________ for biology class.

2.  Microbes are ____________ organisms.

3.  Henry ____________ from high school this spring.

4.  Scientists use ____________ to help people.

5.  You can see very small things with a ____________.

**B  Replace the underlined words with a synonym from the box.**

> miracle    tools    danger    found    badly

1.  Carpenters use many <u>utensils</u> to build things.

2.  The boy was <u>awfully</u> hurt in the bike accident.

3.  It's a <u>wonder</u> they survived the tsunami.

4.  Pandas are in <u>trouble</u>. They might die out.

5.  No one has <u>discovered</u> a cure for the cold.

## Main idea

This story is about ____________.
   a.  World War II
   b.  Jewish doctors
   c.  a scientist's discovery
   d.  the Nobel Prize

## Paragraph Understanding

**Choose the correct answer.**

1. Paragraph ___    Rita had to hide during World War II.
2. Paragraph ___    Rita graduated medical school, but couldn't work.
3. Paragraph ___    Rita found more growth chemicals, and won the Nobel Prize.
4. Paragraph ___    Rita found a growth chemical in her bedroom laboratory.

## Looking for detail

**Circle the correct answer.**

1. Rita did experiments with ___________.
   - a.  needles
   - b.  eggs
   - c.  war
   - d.  burns

2. Growth chemicals are used to ___________.
   - a.  grow fatter
   - b.  make big chickens
   - c.  grow new skin
   - d.  cure cancer

3. Which paragraph talks about the Nazis?
   - a.  Paragraph 1
   - b.  Paragraph 2
   - c.  Paragraph 3
   - d.  Paragraph 4

4. Growth chemicals could be helpful in ___________.
   - a.  growing livers
   - b.  growing into a giant
   - c.  growing more plants
   - d.  growing chickens

## Developing Skills

**Rearrange the words below to make correct sentences.**

1. mind    her    Rita    changed    father's

   _______________________________________

2. bedroom    in    a    set    she    up    laboratory    her

   _______________________________________

3. hid    small    she    apartment    a    in

   _______________________________________

4. things    for    are    the    chemicals    used    many

   _______________________________________

5. won    Nobel    in    Prize    1986    the    Rita

   _______________________________________

### T 16    Summary & Listening Practice

**Read the paragraph and fill in as many blanks as you can.**
**Then listen to the recording and fill in the rest of the blanks.**

Rita Levi-Montalcini had a ① _____________ for science. So, she went to ② _____________ school. Rita was Jewish, and Jewish people weren't allowed to work at many kinds of jobs. She did ③ _____________ in her bedroom. Rita discovered a ④ _____________ that makes ⑤ _____________ grow. After the war, she went to America to work, where she discovered more chemicals. She won the Nobel Prize in 1986.

# Susan Cervantes:
## The Wall Painter



1. Do you like to paint?
2. Have you ever painted on a wall?
3. Do you know what a mural is?

 T 17

1   Most of us think that painters traditionally work on **canvas**. But San Francisco artist Susan Cervantes is a very different kind of painter. She prefers painting on very unusual surfaces likes walls. What's more, she even gets paid to do it. Susan paints **life-sized** wall paintings called **murals**. Most of the time she paints bright and lively scenes.

2   Originally, Susan used to paint on canvas. Then one day, she got tired of looking at the blank wall across the street from her home. It seemed too boring. So she gathered a group of painters to paint a large colorful mural that would cover the whole wall. After that first mural, which livened up the neighborhood, Susan organized the Precita Eyes Mural Arts Center. There she taught other people to paint murals.

3   In fact, mural painting has a long history. Thousands of years ago, **cave** people painted pictures of animals on cave walls. In ancient Egypt and Rome, people decorated the inside of their homes with murals. Today, many murals often reflect different aspects of our culture from street art to gang culture to community projects. When people look at these murals, they can be proud of their history and customs.

4   Murals are often called "people's art" because they are **messages** by the people. They can tell people to do the right thing, to vote, or to love one another. But whatever the message, murals can make any neighborhood more beautiful. For Susan's arts center, promoting mural painting is her way of continuing to make San Francisco more livable.

## Vocabulary Study

**A** Choose and write the correct word.

| life-sized canvas mural cave message |

1. There are many beautiful ___________ s painted on walls.

2. Bears like to sleep in ___________ s during winter.

3. Jane has a ___________ doll. It's as tall as she is.

4. Children like fables because they have a ___________.

5. The artist started to paint on the white ___________.

**B** Replace the underlined words with a synonym from the box.

| traditional bright organized giant proud |

1. The <u>huge</u> sign said, "No Littering!"

2. The room was <u>cheerful</u> and fun.

3. Mrs. Sanders <u>set up</u> an after school drama club.

4. He never gives tests. He's not the <u>usual</u> teacher.

5. Rob's dad was very <u>pleased</u> that Rob won the speech contest.

## Main idea

This story is about ______________.

   a. canvas art             b. history of painting

   c. art on walls            d. writing messages

## Paragraph Understanding

Choose the correct answer.

1. Paragraph ___   Susan and some people painted on a mural on a wall.
2. Paragraph ___   Murals are often called "people's art".
3. Paragraph ___   Susan isn't a traditional painter.
4. Paragraph ___   Mural painting has a long history.

## Looking for detail

Circle the correct answer.

1. Susan Cervantes taught other people how ___________.
   a. to paint on canvas
   b. to paint murals
   c. to paint lively scenes
   d. to paint messages

2. Ancient Egyptians had murals inside their home for ___________.
   a. messages
   b. story-telling
   c. entertainment
   d. decoration

3. Which paragraph talks about murals being messages for people?
   a. Paragraph 1
   b. Paragraph 2
   c. Paragraph 3
   d. Paragraph 4

4. People might paint a mural ___________.
   a. to practice their artistic skills
   b. to organize a mural arts center
   c. to be an art member
   d. to talk about traditional paintings

## Developing Skills

**Rearrange the words below to make correct sentences.**

1. her   Susan   California   lives   in   with   family

   _______________________________________________

2. money   walls   she   paint   gets   on   to

   _______________________________________________

3. murals   about   some   cultures   tell   different

   _______________________________________________

4. neighborhoods   murals   beautiful   make   can

   _______________________________________________

5. animals   cave   painted   people   pictures   of

   _______________________________________________

### 🎧 T 18  Summary & Listening Practice

**Read the paragraph and fill in as many blanks as you can.**
**Then listen to the recording and fill in the rest of the blanks.**

Susan Cervantes paints murals. One day, she got
① ___________ of looking at a boring ② ___________
wall. So, she and some painters painted a
③ ___________ mural on it. Afterwards, Susan created
the Precita Eyes Mural Arts Center. The history of
murals goes back a long time. Cave people,
④ ___________ Egyptians, and even Romans painted
murals. Murals are often called "people's art" because
they are ⑤ ___________ by the people.

 T 19

1   One of the most amazing organs in the body must be our eyes. They are like a camera. Extremely sensitive to light, they can **adjust** to brightness and darkness in an instant. They can focus on distances, far and near, and even see from a wide angle.

2   However, not everyone's eyes work perfectly. Some can't see things far away. Some can't see things too close. When our eyes can't do a perfect job, we have to wear glasses. Unfortunately, there is one problem that even glasses can't correct. That is color blindness.

3   However, the term *color blindness* is a bit misleading. People who are color-blind aren't really "**blind**" to colors. They can see some colors. So color "confusion" would be a better **description**. Actually, the official name for this problem is Daltonism. The name originates from John Dalton, who was the first to study color blindness.

4   There are three different kinds of Daltonism. Confusing yellow with blue is one type. The other two kinds of color confusion are more common. Both types **confuse** red with green. But in one kind, the person can see different shades of red. In the other, the person can see shades of green. Both of these types of Daltonism are typically **inherited**. They seem to be handed down by the mother, even if she isn't color-blind herself.

5   Daltonism can be a problem. But most people with Daltonism live normal lives. They get along just as well as people without the problem. In fact, they may not even know that their world of color is different because they were born that way. That's all they've ever known. All of us have our own world of color. You can't know for sure what someone else sees.

## Vocabulary Study

**A** **Choose and write the correct word.**

> adjust    blind    description    confuse    inherited

1. People ____________ Tom and Tim because they are twins.

2. Helen Keller was deaf and ____________ .

3. It's difficult for children to ____________ to a new school.

4. Sally ____________ her mother's blue eyes.

5. He gave the police a ____________ of the bank robber.

**B** **Replace the underlined words with a synonym from the box.**

> close    correct    official    shades    normal

1. Picasso painted with different <u>hues</u> of blue.

2. The teacher helped him <u>fix</u> his mistakes.

3. We can walk there. The library is <u>near</u>.

4. Most actors have <u>ordinary</u> lives like you and me.

5. The <u>real</u> name of our club is "Friendly Earth".

## Main idea

This story is about ____________ .
   a. about John Dalton      b. color blindness
   c. colors      d. bad eyesight

## Paragraph Understanding

Choose the correct answer.

1. Paragraph ___    Color blindness is actually called Daltonism.
2. Paragraph ___    People with color blindness don't have problems in life.
3. Paragraph ___    There are three different kinds of Daltonism.
4. Paragraph ___    Eyes are extremely sensitive.

## Looking for detail

Circle the correct answer.

1. People who are color-blind ___________.
   a. can see all colors
   b. can see some colors
   c. can't see any colors
   d. only see red and green

2. Two types of color blindness may be ___________.
   a. handed on by the mother
   b. handed on by the father
   c. caused by sickness
   d. inherited from the grandparents

3. Which paragraph talks about what the eyes can do?
   a. Paragraph 1
   b. Paragraph 2
   c. Paragraph 3
   d. Paragraph 4

4. Some people who are color-blind ___________.
   a. may see nothing
   b. inherited it from their sisters
   c. wear glasses to correct it
   d. may not know it

## Developing Skills

**Rearrange the words below to make correct sentences.**

1. to   can   light   adjust   eyes   bright

___________________________________________

2. John Dalton   first   color   blindness   studied

___________________________________________

3. people   green   confuse   some   and   red

___________________________________________

4. Daltonism   most   lives   people   normal   with   live

___________________________________________

5. glasses   help   blindness   can't   color

___________________________________________

### T20　Summary & Listening Practice

**Read the paragraph and fill in as many blanks as you can.**
**Then listen to the recording and fill in the rest of the blanks.**

Eyes are like cameras. But not everyone's eyes work ① ___________. One problem is color blindness. The ② ___________ name for it is Daltonism. There are three different ③ ___________ of Daltonism. Confusing yellow and blue colors is one type. The other two kinds ④ ___________ red and green. These two types may both be ⑤ ___________ from the mother.

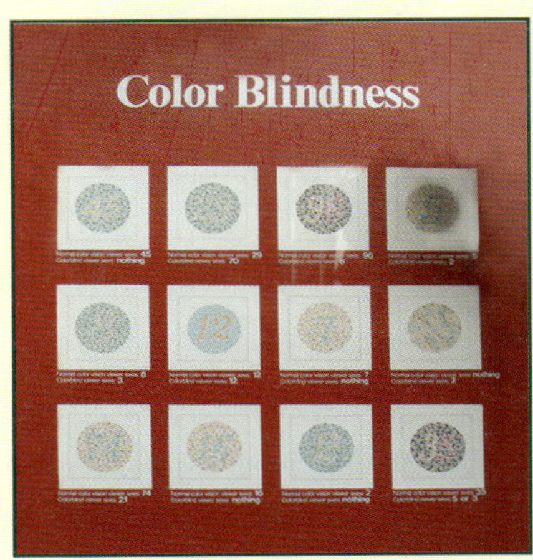

**Pre-reading activity**

1. What's your favorite flower?
2. How many flowers can you name?
3. Do you know what the largest flower in the world is?

 T21

1  Roses, lilies, tulips, and orchids. Flowers delight and amaze us. But do you know what the world's largest flower is? It's the rafflesia or flower lotus. It is usually 36 inches wide and weighs 15 pounds. Some rafflesias even grow to 42 inches! That's as tall as a 5-year-old child. If you want to find one of these rare monster flowers, you will have to travel to the islands in the Pacific Ocean. It only grows in the forests on the islands of Sumatra and Borneo. It has no **roots** or green leaves.

2  What makes the rafflesia unique is that it is a **parasite**. It lives off other plants. One of its greatest dependencies is its reliance on wild grapes. For the flower lotus to grow, it needs the help of others. Small animals like squirrels chew on grape **vines** for food. By chewing, they cut open the vines. Then, insects carry the sticky flower lotus seeds on their bodies. The insects land on the opened vine and the seeds stick to the plant. The growing seed becomes part of the plant, taking food from it.

3  The grape vine doesn't seem to be bothered sharing with the flower lotus. After all, the parasitic flower lotus doesn't hurt the grape vine. About a year and a half later, a flower lotus **bud** pushes through the vine. The bud is about two inches wide and looks like a tiny cabbage. Nine months later, it is ready to bloom.

4  The flower lotus has five bright red leathery **petals**. The petals are covered with raised yellow dots. Hard spikes protect the seeds in the center of the flower. The flower only lives for four days. Then the colorful petals curl up and turn black. After a few weeks, the flower lotus becomes a slimy black mass. And its smell is terrible — like that of a dead animal. Despite the bad smell, it is beneficial. Insects are attracted to the smell, and they carry the seeds to another opened grape vine. Then the cycle begins all over again.

## Vocabulary Study

**A  Choose and write the correct word.**

> roots    parasite    vines    bud    petals

1. The gardener sees a tiny ____________ pushing through the ground.

2. Trees have long, strong ____________ under the ground.

3. The ____________ of the flower are falling off.

4. A tapeworm is a kind of ____________. It lives off others.

5. Tarzan likes to swing on ____________ in the jungle.

**B  Replace the underlined words with a synonym from the box.**

> rare    sticky    bothered    blooms    leathery

1. Honey is very <u>gluey</u> when it gets on your hands.

2. The cowboy's hands were very <u>rough</u>.

3. A purple diamond is <u>uncommon</u> in the world.

4. The plant <u>opens</u> for only one week in spring.

5. She <u>annoyed</u> her brother by being noisy.

## Main idea

This story is about ____________.
- a. the flower lotus
- b. grape vines
- c. parasites
- d. insects

## Paragraph Understanding

Choose the correct answer.

1. Paragraph ____    The rafflesia is the biggest flower in the world.
2. Paragraph ____    The flower lives for only four days and then turns black.
3. Paragraph ____    A flower lotus bud looks like a tiny cabbage.
4. Paragraph ____    The flower lotus needs grape vines, animals and insects to live.

## Looking for detail

Circle the correct answer.

1. A 5-year-old child is about ____________.
   a. 36 inches tall
   b. 42 inches tall
   c. 15 inches tall
   d. 15 pounds

2. The flower lotus has petals that are covered with ____________.
   a. black slime
   b. leather
   c. dead animals
   d. raised yellow dots

3. Which paragraph talks about the flower lotus after it blooms?
   a. Paragraph 1
   b. Paragraph 2
   c. Paragraph 3
   d. Paragraph 4

4. If grape vines couldn't live in Sumatra and Borneo, then ____________.
   a. squirrels would all die
   b. the flower lotus would disappear
   c. insects couldn't eat the seeds
   d. the flower lotus would be small

## Developing Skills

**Find a grammatical mistake and correct it.**

1. The flower lotus only grow in Sumatra and Borneo.

_______________________________________________

2. The rafflesia don't have green leaves.

_______________________________________________

3. Animals chew but cut open the vine.

_______________________________________________

4. The flower lotus has red five petals.

_______________________________________________

5. It looks and smells alike a dead animal.

_______________________________________________

---

### T22  Summary & Listening Practice

**Read the paragraph and fill in as many blanks as you can.**
**Then listen to the recording and fill in the rest of the blanks.**

The world's largest flower is the flower lotus, sometimes ① _____________ as
the rafflesia. It only grows on the islands of Sumatra and Borneo. It is
② ____________ on the grape vine to live. Small animals ③ ____________ and
open the grape vines. Insects carry the flower lotus seeds to the opened
grape vines. Soon, the seeds become part of
the plant. After, a flower ④ ____________ . The
flower dies four days later and turns black.
Later, the plant smells like a dead animal.
Insects come and carry the seeds. Then the
⑤ ____________ starts again.

# 12  The Quagga – A Sad Story

 T23

1. We've all heard of blue whales, Siberian tigers and African elephants as magnificent rare animals. All of them are in danger of going **extinct**. That means that they are dangerously close to dying out. For decades, humankind has been destroying their habitats and killing them. Many **hunters** would kill elephants for their ivory tusks. Tigers were hunted for their fur coats. Now there are animal groups trying to protect **endangered** animals. But one mammal, the quagga, couldn't get their help.

2. The quagga was the size of a small horse and looked like a weird kind of zebra. It was light brown, with stripes only on its head, neck, and front. A dark brown line ran down the middle of its back. It had the ears and tail of a donkey. Its legs were white with black hoofs. The quagga made a strange noise. It sounded like, "KWA-guh." That's how it got its name.

3. Herds of quagga once ran free over the plains of South Africa. Then settlers from Europe moved to South Africa in the 1600s. Although they didn't like the taste of quagga meat, their workers thought it was delicious. Quaggas were easy to hunt and the settlers could cheaply feed their workforce. The **hides** of the quagga were also useful for making sacks and shoes. The settlers killed hundreds and hundreds of quaggas.

4. Since quaggas were wild animals, they could be easily **tamed**. It would have been simple to raise them for meat and skins just as cows are raised. But no one thought of that. People just kept on hunting and killing them. Eventually, their numbers dwindled so much in 1873, and there was only one quagga alive in the entire world. A zoo in the Netherlands had the last female quagga. The lone quagga finally died in 1883. It was a tragic ending for an unusual animal that humankind had destroyed.

## Vocabulary Study

**A  Choose and write the correct word.**

| extinct | endangered | hunt | hides | tamed |
|---|---|---|---|---|

1. Sadly, many animals are ___________.

2. Cow ___________ are used for making leather goods.

3. Monkeys can be ___________ as pets.

4. Dinosaurs died out a long time ago. They are ___________.

5. It's illegal to ___________ elephants in Africa.

**B  Replace the underlined words with a synonym from the box.**

| habitats | unfinished | useful | wild | entire |
|---|---|---|---|---|

1. <u>Untamed</u> boars are extremely violent.

2. People are destroying the <u>environments</u> of many animals.

3. The house was <u>incomplete</u> without a roof.

4. Dan ate the <u>whole</u> pie by himself.

5. The website gives very <u>helpful</u> information.

## Main idea

This story is about ___________.

a. the extinction of quaggas     b. different kinds of zebras

c. the taming of animals     d. European settlers

## Paragraph Understanding

**Choose the correct answer.**

1. Paragraph ____    Many animals are endangered.
2. Paragraph ____    The settlers killed quaggas for their meat and hide.
3. Paragraph ____    The last quagga died in 1883.
4. Paragraph ____    The quagga looked like half a zebra.

## Looking for detail

**Circle the correct answer.**

1. The quagga had ears like a ____________.
   a. donkey                         b. zebra
   c. horse                          d. tiger

2. The quagga made a noise ____________.
   a. that was pretty                b. that sounded like its name
   c. that scared people away        d. that was like a donkey's bray

3. Which paragraph talks about endangered tigers?
   a. Paragraph 1                    b. Paragraph 2
   c. Paragraph 3                    d. Paragraph 4

4. If the settlers had tamed the quaggas, then ____________.
   a. they would still exist today
   b. they would be used like donkeys
   c. they would live in zoos
   d. they would make a different noise

## Developing Skills

**Find a grammatical mistake and correct it.**

1. Tigers were hunt for their fur.

   ___________________________________________

2. The animal was the size as a small horse.

   ___________________________________________

3. A dark brown line ran down it's back.

   ___________________________________________

4. They ran free under the plains of South Africa.

   ___________________________________________

5. On 1873 there was only one quagga left.

   ___________________________________________

 T 24    **Summary & Listening Practice**

**Read the paragraph and fill in as many blanks as you can. Then listen to the recording and fill in the rest of the blanks.**

① ____________, animal groups are trying to protect ② ____________ animals. But the quaggas weren't so lucky. The quagga looked like an ③ ____________ zebra. It made a noise that ④ ____________ like its name. In the 1600s, Europeans ⑤ ____________ in South Africa and hunted the quaggas. They killed so many that by 1873, there was only one left. It died in 1883 in a zoo in the Netherlands.

# Crash-test Dummies Save Lives

 T 25

1. There are about 20 million car **crashes** in the U.S. every year. That's more than the entire populations of many European countries. Sadly, these **accidents** kill about 40,000 Americans. Fortunately, the situation is getting a little better. Of course, most of us wear **seat belts** and there are driving laws to help save many lives. But the deaths continue, even though fewer car-accident related deaths are happening for each mile of driving. So how to fight these senseless fatalities? Well, dummies might just be the answer.

2. Before a car is sold to the public, it is crashed into concrete walls. This is done on purpose by carmakers who crash the cars to test the **safety** features. Many crash tests are performed using one car. They also crash special "sleds" designed like the insides of cars. The most important part of these tests is plastic dummies, used since the 1950s.

3. Crash test dummies are modeled after real human bodies. They are made in different sizes and weights to simulate real men, women, and children. There are even pregnant dummies. They have arms, legs, and heads just like real people. Their "bones" and "joints" move like real body parts. Dummies even wear clothes to show how a person slides on the seat during an accident.

4. Each crash test dummy is connected with special wires to a computer. In a crash test, the computer measures more than 30 different factors. During a crash test, all 30 factors are measured 4,000 times. **Engineers** continue to make new designs for crash test dummies. Each process using up-to-date dummies helps the models to act more like real human bodies. This should result in safer cars for us all.

## Vocabulary Study

**A  Choose and write the correct word.**

| seat belts | safety | crash | accident | engineers |
|---|---|---|---|---|

1.  Joe got into an ____________, but he's okay.

2.  The plane is now departing. Please fasten your ____________.

3.  Stay away from the sliding doors for your ____________.

4.  The ____________ won an award for designing the bridge.

5.  Be careful! Don't ____________ into the wall.

**B  Replace the underlined words with a synonym from the box.**

| sadly | on purpose | special | up-to-date | act |
|---|---|---|---|---|

1.  Gorillas <u>behave</u> a lot like humans.

2.  Stage actors wear <u>unique</u> make-up on stage.

3.  <u>Unfortunately</u>, Lisa can't come to the party.

4.  Channel 5 gives <u>current</u> news every hour.

5.  She didn't step on your foot <u>deliberately</u>.

## Main idea

This story is about ____________.

    a.  cars        b.  carmakers

    c.  crash test dummies        d.  crashes

## Paragraph Understanding

**Choose the correct answer.**

1. Paragraph ____     Carmakers crash cars to make them safer.
2. Paragraph ____     Engineers keep making new crash-test dummies.
3. Paragraph ____     Less people are dying in car accidents.
4. Paragraph ____     Dummies are made to be like real people.

## Looking for detail

**Circle the correct answer.**

1. Seat belts ____________.
   - a. help save lives
   - b. don't do anything
   - c. are never worn
   - d. are uncomfortable

2. The computer measures ____________.
   - a. 3 factors, 4,000 times
   - b. 30 factors, 400 times
   - c. 30 factors, 4,000 times
   - d. 4 factors, 30 times

3. Which paragraph talks about the different kinds of crash-test dummies?
   - a. Paragraph 1
   - b. Paragraph 2
   - c. Paragraph 3
   - d. Paragraph 4

4. Dummies that are more like humans ____________.
   - a. help make cars safer
   - b. fit into clothes better
   - c. move more naturally
   - d. can slide better on the seat

## Developing Skills

**Find a grammatical mistake and correct it.**

1. Car crashes kills about 40,000 people every year.

2. Dummies are made be like real people.

3. They can build cars that are even safe than before.

4. Engineers do much crash tests with one car.

5. Dummies were used in tests for the 1950s.

### T 26　　Summary & Listening Practice

**Read the paragraph and fill in as many blanks as you can.**
**Then listen to the recording and fill in the rest of the blanks.**

Many car accidents ① ＿＿＿＿＿＿ every year. One of the best ways to improve the safety of everyone's lives is to use crash test dummies to ② ＿＿＿＿＿ humans. Carmakers crash cars into concrete walls to see the ③ ＿＿＿＿＿. Crash test dummies are used to see how safe the car is for people. They are modeled after real human bodies, even ④ ＿＿＿＿＿ women. Through wires, they are connected to a computer. The computer takes special ⑤ ＿＿＿＿＿. Engineers want models that act more like real people.

# 14 The Williams Sisters

 T 27

1   There's nothing like the suspenseful ending in sports between two evenly matched competitors. During the 1998 Australian Open tennis **tournament**, Serena Williams, at the young age of 16, was playing in the second round. It was her first Grand Slam singles event. In the first round, she started to win, but then started losing. Her taller, older **opponent** was beating her. Finally, the match ended. Serena jumped over the net and congratulated the winner. The winner was Venus Williams, Serena's sister.

2   That year, the Williams sisters were rising stars in women's tennis. These young up-and-coming champions received a lot of media attention because they were sisters. What was even more unusual was that they had to **compete** in the same match together. But the main reason for their stardom was because of their talent. Venus was **ranked** the seventh-best player in the world. Serena was ranked number 30. And this was only five months after she had played her first tournament!

3   Many people are amazed that the Williams sisters have come so far in the highly competitive world of tennis. The two sisters were raised in a poor community near Los Angeles, California. Tennis is often viewed as a sport for the elites of society. Most young tennis players learn the game from professional coaches at private clubs. But Venus and Serena learned to play in public parks. Their **coach** was their father, Richard, who had learned the game of tennis from reading books.

4   When she was 14, Venus Williams turned pro. A few years later, Serena Williams turned pro as well. In 1999, Serena won the US Open and became the first sister to win a Grand Slam event. The next year, it was Venus's turn. She won the 2000 Wimbledon title. Venus and Serena also paired up that year to win the Wimbledon doubles title. Since then, Venus and Serena Williams have been two of the most dominant players in women's tennis.

## Vocabulary Study

**A  Choose and write the correct word.**

> tournament    opponent    compete    ranked    coach

1.  The song ____________ number 1 on the Billboard music charts.

2.  Carl's ___________ was a more experienced chess player.

3.  The ___________ jumped into the air when his team won.

4.  Mandy will ___________ in a dance contest.

5.  The team is nervous about the ___________.

**B  Replace the underlined words with a synonym from the box.**

> stardom   amazed   community   professional   dominant

1.  It's a very safe and quiet neighborhood.

2.  He rose to popularity in only one year.

3.  Tiger Woods is an experienced golfer.

4.  Michael Jordan was the most powerful player in his day.

5.  The 5-year-old kid surprised everyone with her vivid paintings.

## Main idea

This story is about _______________.
    a.  two twin sisters              b.  a great coach
    c.  stars on TV                   d.  star tennis players

## Paragraph Understanding

Choose the correct answer.

1. Paragraph ____    The Williams sisters became tennis stars.
2. Paragraph ____    Venus beat Serena in a Grand Slam event.
3. Paragraph ____    They learned tennis from their father.
4. Paragraph ____    Serena won the first Grand Slam event, then Venus.

## Looking for detail

Circle the correct answer.

1. In 1998, Venus was ranked ____________.
   a.  30th                                    b.  7th
   c.  1st                                     d.  3rd

2. Venus and Serena won the Wimbledon doubles title in ____________.
   a.  1998                                    b.  1999
   c.  2000                                    d.  2001

3. Which paragraph talks about the 1998 Australian Open tennis tournament?
   a.  Paragraph 1                             b.  Paragraph 2
   c.  Paragraph 3                             d.  Paragraph 4

4. Many people probably like watching the Williams play because ____________.
   a.  they're are bad                         b.  they're beautiful
   c.  they're are poor                        d.  they're highly talented

## Developing Skills

**Find a grammatical mistake and correct it.**

1. Serena jumped over the net but congratulated the winner.

   _______________________________________________________

2. They were getting a lots of attention.

   _______________________________________________________

3. The two sisters grew in a poor community.

   _______________________________________________________

4. Richard learned tennis at a book.

   _______________________________________________________

5. Venus turned pro where she was 14.

   _______________________________________________________

### T28    Summary & Listening Practice

**Read the paragraph and fill in as many blanks as you can.**
**Then listen to the recording and fill in the rest of the blanks.**

During the 1998 Australian Open, Serena lost to her sister, Venus. This was the year that they both became very ① _____________. At the time, Venus was ranked 7th, and Serena was ranked 30th. The sisters grew up in a poor ② ___________ near L.A. They practiced in public parks, not at ③ ___________ clubs. In addition, their father was their coach. They both turned ④ ___________ and won Grand Slam ⑤ ___________.

# 15 Smart Buildings

 T 29

1. One of the most destructive forces on earth comes from a big **earthquake**. This is when the earth **shakes** and cracks form. If you've ever seen a movie where a city is hit by an earthquake, it looks pretty scary. The ground opens up, the earth shakes, and tall buildings fall down. Sounds scary, right? Unfortunately, this can happen in real life. Buildings that were built under old regulations are especially vulnerable during an earthquake because they are not so strong.

2. Nowadays, tall buildings are called **skyscrapers**. But it's these buildings that worry engineers the most. In order to make them safer during earthquakes, scientists and engineers are researching better ways to design them. Many of these new skyscrapers have been nicknamed "smart" buildings. These modern smart buildings keep standing even during a major earthquake. During an earthquake, the people inside can hardly feel any shaking at all. They are built to actually move back and forth a little bit during an earthquake. They move in the opposite direction of the shaking.

3. There are three ways that these smart buildings do this. Some buildings have huge weights in them. The weights glide back and forth during an earthquake. They help the building to stabilize and **balance** itself. Other engineers have created buildings that use strong metal ropes or braces. These pull the building back into position if it moves off center. The third way is to use jets of water or air to push the building back into place.

4. All three ways are guided by special computers. These computers can feel or sense the slightest shaking. They are programmed to **react** in less than a second to adjust the building back to its correct position. The amazing thing is that when these movements happen, the people inside the building probably don't even feel it. These smart buildings save lives now because we have smart people building them!

## Vocabulary Study

**A  Choose and write the correct word.**

| earthquake | shakes | skyscrapers | balance | react |

1.  New York City has many ____________ like the Empire State Building.

2.  A strong ____________ can destroy a whole village.

3.  Ballerinas must learn how to ____________ on their toes.

4.  Ned ____________ the tree to get some apples.

5.  The police must ____________ fast in an emergency.

**B  Replace the underlined words with a synonym from the box.**

| old-fashioned | major | smart | sense | slightest |

1.  The <u>smallest</u> sound will wake her up.

2.  The little boy looked very <u>intelligent</u>.

3.  Your thinking is <u>outdated</u>. You have to think in the future.

4.  I <u>feel</u> that the teacher is angry.

5.  We're having a <u>big</u> test tomorrow.

## Main idea

This story is about ______________ .
   a.  tall buildings
   b.  good designs
   c.  earthquakes
   d.  moving buildings

## Paragraph Understanding

**Choose the correct answer.**

1. Paragraph ____    "Smart" buildings actually move during earthquakes.
2. Paragraph ____    Earthquakes can make tall buildings fall down.
3. Paragraph ____    Computers put the buildings in their correct positions.
4. Paragraph ____    Weights, metal ropes, and jets of air keep buildings balanced.

## Looking for detail

**Circle the correct answer.**

1. "Smart" buildings move ____________.
   a. in the opposite direction of shakes
   b. in the same direction of shakes
   c. in a circular motion
   d. in an up and down motion

2. ____________ glide back and forth in smart buildings.
   a. a. braces                    b. water
   c. weights                      d. skyscrapers

3. Which paragraph talks about the three ways smart buildings move?
   a. Paragraph 1                  b. Paragraph 2
   c. Paragraph 3                  d. Paragraph 4

4. During an earthquake, people in a smart building probably ________.
   a. wouldn't feel it             b. wouldn't move
   c. would worry                  d. would feel the shakes

## Developing Skills

### Find a grammatical mistake and correct it.

1. Extremely tall building are called skyscrapers.

   _________________________________________________

2. Smart buildings can keep standing even during major earthquake.

   _________________________________________________

3. Weights help the building to balance herself.

   _________________________________________________

4. All three ways guided by special computers.

   _________________________________________________

5. Buildings that have been build long ago may be unsafe.

   _________________________________________________

 T 30
## Summary & Listening Practice

### Read the paragraph and fill in as many blanks as you can.
### Then listen to the recording and fill in the rest of the blanks.

Each year, scientists and engineers are finding better ways to build tall buildings. Many of these buildings are designed to keep standing even during a ① ___________ earthquake. They have been ② ___________ "smart" buildings. When the building shakes, they move in the ③ ___________ direction. The buildings use weights, strong ④ ___________ ropes, and jets of water or air to keep the building from falling down. Special computers act fast to ⑤ ___________ the building's position.

 T31

1. There is nothing more **serene** and relaxing than enjoying a beautiful garden. Well trimmed bushes, multi-colored plants and the beautiful smell of fresh flowers. More than anything else, flower gardens provide beauty for all to see. Additionally, vegetable gardens give us delicious food to eat. But did you know that taking care of a garden can also make us healthier?

2. In the United States, about 80% of all families do some form of gardening. Some people have gardens in the front or back of their homes. Others have a small window garden in their apartments. So why do so many people garden? Well, scientists who study the way people think and feel say that gardening has a special effect on us. Here are some fascinating things about it.

3. Gardening helps us relax! People who spend time planting, watering, and weeding a garden feel better about themselves. It seems that gardening has a relaxing effect, giving people a chance to calm down from their busy lives. Gardeners enjoy the colors and **scents** of the various flowers. The **soil** running through their hands even feels good. All this makes gardeners feel close to **nature**. Most of all, there is a sense of accomplishment when they finish planting their garden and they see the beautiful results of their work.

4. But is there any **scientific** relation between gardening and relaxing? Scientists found that when people feel better about themselves, they also feel better in general. So, they are less likely to get sick. However, gardens have an additional benefit. They can also help people who are already ill. One scientist discovered that hospital patients who have a garden outside their window get better more quickly. Basically, growing beautiful and healthy things in the garden makes us beautiful and healthy, too!

## Vocabulary Study

**A  Choose and write the correct word.**

| serene | scents | scientific | soil | nature |
| --- | --- | --- | --- | --- |

1.  Put some ___________ into the pot, and then add the seeds.

2.  Let's go to the country and enjoy ___________.

3.  We were impressed by the ___________ beauty of the village.

4.  In fact, ___________ methods are very powerful.

5.  She loves the different ___________ of perfume.

**B  Replace the underlined words with a synonym from the box.**

| form | affect | fascinating | accomplishment | ill |
| --- | --- | --- | --- | --- |

1.  Being the president of your own company is an <u>achievement</u>.

2.  Classical music has an <u>influence</u> on babies.

3.  The roller coaster ride made me <u>sick</u>.

4.  You have to do some <u>kind</u> of exercise to stay healthy.

5.  The article about space travel was <u>interesting</u>.

## Main idea

This story is about ______________.
- a.  the benefits of gardening
- b.  mother nature
- c.  the beauty of flowers
- d.  stress and health

## Paragraph Understanding

**Choose the correct answer.**

1. Paragraph ___    Sick people get better faster when they have gardens.
2. Paragraph ___    Gardening helps people relax and feel better about themselves.
3. Paragraph ___    80% of Americans have gardens or grow plants in pots.
4. Paragraph ___    People enjoy gardens for their flowers and vegetables.

## Looking for detail

**Circle the correct answer.**

1. Gardeners feel close to ___________.
   a. people
   b. soil
   c. nature
   d. health

2. People who garden are ___________.
   a. less likely to get sick
   b. more stressed
   c. usually ill
   d. very busy

3. Which paragraph talks about America families?
   a. Paragraph 1
   b. Paragraph 2
   c. Paragraph 3
   d. Paragraph 4

4. People who have gardens are probably ___________.
   a. very sick and in the hospital
   b. too busy to take care of them
   c. less stressed than people who don't
   d. lonely and bored with life

## Developing Skills

**Find a grammatical mistake and correct it.**

1. Vegetable gardens give our delicious food to eat.

   ___________________________________________________________

2. People which spend time planting feel better about themselves.

   ___________________________________________________________

3. They can calm down from there busy lives.

   ___________________________________________________________

4. Gardeners are lesser likely to get sick.

   ___________________________________________________________

5. Some people grow plants on pots.

   ___________________________________________________________

### T 32   Summary & Listening Practice

**Read the paragraph and fill in as many blanks as you can.**
**Then listen to the recording and fill in the rest of the blanks.**

Gardens are very important to our health. Many people in the U.S. have a garden. Scientists think there is a ① ___________ between gardening and ② ___________ from a busy day. When people garden, they can enjoy the colors and ③ ___________ of the flowers, including the feel of the soil in their hands. They feel close to nature and also a sense of ④ ___________ . Having a garden even helps hospital ⑤ ___________ get better faster.

T33

1   Of all the rumors about monsters that have circulated throughout history, one case must be the most amazing. The world's last remaining monster is supposed to live in the deep blue waters of the Scottish lake Loch Ness. Or does it? The monster is called Nessie, and it was first **spotted** over 1,400 years ago. According to legend, Nessie was going to kill a swimmer. Then Saint Columba appeared and cried out, "Do not touch that man!" The giant lake monster with red eyes as long as a dinosaur swam away.

2   The Loch Ness monster wasn't heard of again until the 1930s. People began telling stories about seeing Nessie. Then a photograph was taken in 1934 by a doctor who supposedly saw the monster stick its head above the water. It showed a strange **creature** with a small head and a long, thin neck. It almost looked like an ancient dinosaur. But the picture wasn't **clear**. Some people weren't sure what the picture really showed.

3   The story of Nessie became so popular that in 1969, a team of scientists decided to **investigate**. They used sonar to help them. Sonar is a kind of radar that uses sound waves to find objects underwater. One day, on August 8th, the sonar machine began beeping. Weird **signals** appeared on the sonar monitor. The scientists realized that the signals showed not one, but two sea monsters! Yet in the 1980s, another sonar search showed no results.

4   Do the sightings, pictures, and sonar signals prove that there really is a monster in Loch Ness? Some people believe there is. But some aren't so certain. Many say Nessie is just a myth. What do you think? The waters of Loch Ness are very dark and deep. Does a monster live there? The truth may never be known.

## Vocabulary Study

**A  Choose and write the correct word.**

| spotted    creature    clear    investigate    signals |

1.  The scientist discovered a new ____________ in the rainforest.

2.  The detective must ____________ the case.

3.  A UFO was ____________ flying above the mountains.

4.  The picture is nice and ____________. I can see everything.

5.  The machine showed ____________ of a large animal.

**B  Replace the underlined words with a synonym from the box.**

| appeared    weird    certain    thin    myth |

1.  Melanie's brother is really tall and skinny.

2.  The insect makes a very odd sound at night.

3.  Some scientists say Bigfoot is only a legend.

4.  Your brother showed up at the meeting.

5.  The weather forecaster is positive that it will snow.

## Main idea

This story is about ____________.

a.  monsters                    b.  Nessie

c.  Scotland                    d.  a lake

## Paragraph Understanding

**Choose the correct answer.**

1. Paragraph ____     Scientists used sonar to find the monster.
2. Paragraph ____     Nessie was spotted by Saint Columba.
3. Paragraph ____     Some people believe in Nessie, and some don't.
4. Paragraph ____     A doctor took a picture of something that looked like a dinosaur.

## Looking for detail

**Circle the correct answer.**

1. The Loch Ness monster was first seen ____________.
   - a. over 14 years ago
   - b. over 40 years ago
   - c. over 400 years ago
   - d. over 1,400 years ago

2. In 1969, sonar signals showed ___________.
   - a. 2 sea monsters
   - b. 1 sea monster
   - c. no sea monsters
   - d. 3 sea monsters

3. Which paragraph talks about a picture of Nessie?
   - a. Paragraph 1
   - b. Paragraph 2
   - c. Paragraph 3
   - d. Paragraph 4

4. It will probably be difficult to prove if Nessie exists or not because ___________.
   - a. sonar machines don't work
   - b. no one wants to investigate
   - c. the lake is very dark and deep
   - d. people are afraid of Nessie

## Developing Skills

### Find a grammatical mistake and correct it.

1. Nessie were going to kill a swimmer.

________________________________________

2. People weren't sure which the picture showed.

________________________________________

3. Sonar uses sound waves find objects underwater.

________________________________________

4. On August 8rd the sonar began beeping.

________________________________________

5. A second sonar search showed any results.

________________________________________

## T 34　Summary & Listening Practice

**Read the paragraph and fill in as many blanks as you can. Then listen to the recording and fill in the rest of the blanks.**

The Loch Ness monster, ① ____________ as Nessie, was first seen more than 1,400 years ago. In 1934, a doctor took a picture of the monster in the Scottish lake. It looked like a ② ____________. But the picture wasn't clear. Later, a team of scientists used sonar ③ ____________ to find the monster. The sonar showed two sea monsters. However, years later, another sonar ④ ____________ showed nothing. Some people believe in Nessie. Others think it's just a ⑤ ____________.

**Pre-reading activity**
1. Do know what ozone is?
2. Why do you think the ozone layer is important?
3. What do you think may be harmful to the ozone layer?

 T 35

1   Ozone is part of the **atmosphere** that helps protect the Earth's environment. It's a form of oxygen gas that is extremely useful because it **blocks** the sun's harmful **ultraviolet rays**. It also lets in warmth and light. About 90% of all ozone exists as a thin layer in the upper atmosphere. It's about 15 miles above the earth. If this layer becomes thinner, ultraviolet rays would no longer be blocked from reaching the surface of the Earth. This would lead to more people with skin cancer and eye problems. Basically, all living things on earth would be affected, including animals, forests, and oceans.

2   To the shock of scientists in 1986, a "hole" was discovered in the ozone layer. People soon started to worry about the future of the planet. Scientists researched the problem, and found what caused the hole. The **ozone layer** was being **damaged** by chemicals. One of those chemicals was called CFCs. It was commonly used in refrigerators and air conditioners. The other kinds of chemicals were used to fight fires or to kill bad insects.

3   Although these chemicals were useful in many ways, they destroyed the ozone layer very quickly. The chemicals destroyed ozone faster than nature could replace it. So, in 1987 in Montreal, many countries agreed to cut their use of those chemicals in half. However, it didn't seem to help. The damage continued to spread.

4   When scientists first discovered the ozone hole, it was over the South Pole. By the early 1990s, the ozone layer had started to become thinner over more populated places like parts of North America, Asia, and Australia. The countries that signed the original agreement met again to finally solve the problem. This time, they agreed to completely stop making the chemicals by 1996. Because of these efforts, much of the hole in the ozone layer has been repaired. It is estimated that it will be closed for good by 2050.

## Vocabulary Study

**A  Choose and write the correct word.**

> blocks   atmosphere   ultraviolet rays   ozone layer   damaged

1. Put some sunscreen on. It ____________ the UV rays.

2. Children should learn more about the ____________ .

3. There was a lot of heat as the comet entered the earth's ____________ .

4. ____________ can cause skin cancer.

5. The scooter was ____________ after the accident.

**B  Replace the underlined words with a synonym from the box.**

> harmful      cut      spread      original      for good

1. Let's take a look at the <u>first</u> designs.

2. They tried to <u>reduce</u> costs by using coupons.

3. George decided to quit smoking <u>forever</u>.

4. Eating too much sugar is <u>unhealthy</u>.

5. The problem continued to <u>escalate</u>.

## Main idea

This story is about ____________ .

  a.  the ozone layer          b.  ultraviolet rays

  c.  CFCs                     d.  the atmosphere

## Paragraph Understanding

**Choose the correct answer.**

1. Paragraph ____    Countries agreed to stop making harmful chemicals.
2. Paragraph ____    Countries agreed to use less of the chemicals.
3. Paragraph ____    The ozone layer protects us from harmful rays.
4. Paragraph ____    Scientists discovered a hole in the ozone layer.

## Looking for detail

**Circle the correct answer.**

1. About ____________ of ozone is a thin layer.
   - a. 10%
   - b. 90%
   - c. 100%
   - d. 80%

2. CFCs are used in ____________ .
   - a. air conditioners
   - b. fire extinguishers
   - c. insect sprays
   - d. electric fans

3. Which paragraph talks about the ozone layer over Asia and Australia?
   - a. Paragraph 1
   - b. Paragraph 2
   - c. Paragraph 3
   - d. Paragraph 4

4. Since 1996, the levels of harmful chemicals in the ozone layer ________ .
   - a. have probably stayed the same
   - b. have probably disappeared
   - c. have probably decreased
   - d. have probably increased

## Developing Skills

**Find a grammatical mistake and correct it.**

1.  The layer is about 15 mile above the earth.

2.  The whole in the ozone layer worried people.

3.  The ozone layer was been damaged by chemicals.

4.  The chemicals destroyed the ozone layer quick.

5.  This efforts may help close the hole in the ozone layer.

 T 36

## Summary & Listening Practice

**Read the paragraph and fill in as many blanks as you can.**
**Then listen to the recording and fill in the rest of the blanks.**

Part of the Earth's upper atmosphere ① ___________ of ozone that helps block harmful ultraviolet rays. In 1986, scientists discovered a hole in the ozone layer. The hole was ② ___________ by chemicals. The chemicals were used in refrigerators and air ③ ___________. They were also used to fight fires or to kill insects. Although the chemicals were ④ ___________, they were very harmful to the ozone layer. So, many countries agreed to cut their use in half. It didn't help. Then they agreed to ⑤ ___________ stop making the chemicals by 1996.

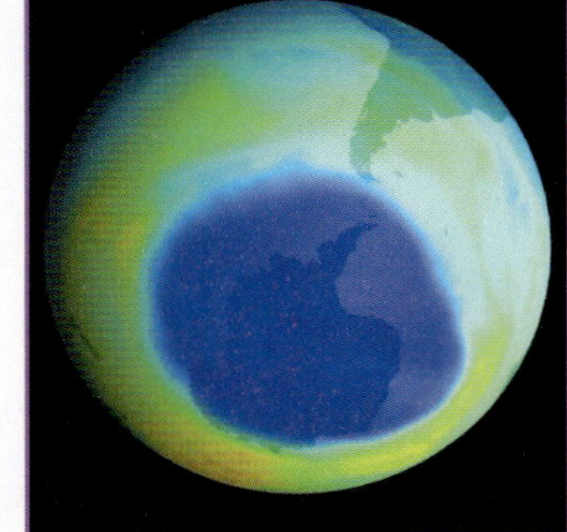

# Giant Otters

 T37

1    There are cute and ugly animals, dangerous and timid animals, and fast and slow animals. But one of the most interesting animals must be the loveable otter. We all know about sea otters from going to the zoo, but did you know there are also giant otters? The giant otter lives in the rivers of South America. With sleek bodies, tiny ears, and long tails, the giant otter looks much like its smaller cousins in the United States. However, the giant otter is much bigger, measuring six feet long and weighs up to 70 pounds! Another difference is while most otters live and hunt alone, giant otters live and work together.

2    Giant otters live in groups to **survive**. The rain forests of South America can be dangerous. Many snakes, jaguars, and alligators roam the rivers for **prey**. A lone otter would make an easy target for food. But in groups of six to eight animals, the giant otters can protect themselves.

3    Sometimes, acting as a team, they can even kill and eat jaguars and alligators! When giant otters meet an alligator in the water, they surround and confuse it. Then two or three of them swim under the alligator. With their sharp **claws**, they slash open its soft belly. Occasionally, they do hunt larger animals, but giant otters live mostly on a diet of fish. While fishing, the otters work together, too. They swim in a line, and herd the fish into shallow water. Then they are easier to catch.

4    Living in groups has another benefit as well. It makes it easier for giant otters to care for their young. All the adult otters participate in raising the young otter **cubs**. Each adult takes turns watching the cubs while the others fish. Young otters watch the adults and copy their hunting techniques. In this way, they learn how to **cooperate** and be a team player. When they grow up, they will know how to act as a group.

## Vocabulary Study

**A  Choose and write the correct word.**

| survive | prey | claws | cubs | cooperate |

1.  Tigers have very long and sharp ____________ .

2.  Mountaineers have to be able to ____________ the harsh weather.

3.  We'll finish faster if we ____________ with one another.

4.  Eagles swoop down to catch their ____________ .

5.  Don't be fooled by bear ____________ . They're stronger than they look.

**B  Replace the underlined words with a synonym from the box.**

| sleek | protect | slash | shallow | copy |

1.  Ralph, Cindy's dog, will always <u>guard</u> her.

2.  Don't be afraid. Come in the pool. The <u>bottom end</u> is not that bad.

3.  The woman had long, <u>smooth</u> hair.

4.  Some kid tried to <u>cut</u> my tires!

5.  Monkeys can <u>mimic</u> human behavior.

## Main idea

This story is about ____________ .
  a.  giant otters
  b.  hunting animals
  c.  American otters
  d.  playing on a team

## Paragraph Understanding

Choose the correct answer.

1. Paragraph ___   Giant otters can kill and eat jaguars and alligators.
2. Paragraph ___   All the adults take turns watching the cubs.
3. Paragraph ___   Giant otters can be six feet long and weigh 70 pounds.
4. Paragraph ___   They hunt together in a group to catch food more easily.

## Looking for detail

Circle the correct answer.

1. When giant otters hunt alligators, they use their ___________.
   a.  claws                    b.  teeth
   c.  tails                    d.  bellies

2. ___________ adult otters participate in raising the young otter cubs.
   a.  3                        b.  2
   c.  1                        d.  All

3. Which paragraph talks about how giant otters fish?
   a.  Paragraph 1              b.  Paragraph 2
   c.  Paragraph 3              d.  Paragraph 4

4. If giant otters didn't live in groups, then they would probably ___________.
   a.  move to America          b.  be killed and eaten
   c.  find another food source d.  change their diet

## Developing Skills

**Find a grammatical mistake and correct it.**

1.  In groups the giant otters can protect itself.

   _______________________________________________

2.  Two and three of them swim under the animal.

   _______________________________________________

3.  Giant otters live mostly in a diet of fish.

   _______________________________________________

4.  Living in groups has other benefit as well.

   _______________________________________________

5.  They learn how be a team player.

   _______________________________________________

### T38  Summary & Listening Practice

**Read the paragraph and fill in as many blanks as you can.**
**Then listen to the recording and fill in the rest of the blanks.**

① _____________ for its size, the South American giant otter looks much like its smaller cousins from the U.S. But giant otters are much bigger. They also live in groups. In groups of six to eight otters, they can even kill and eat jaguars and alligators. Even though they sometimes hunt larger animals, giant otters ② _____________ live on fish. They work together while fishing, too. But one of the biggest ③ _____________ of living in groups is raising their ④ _____________ together. They take turns watching the ⑤ _____________.

# The Cliff Dwellers

 T 39

1   Of all the places to build a home, caves must seem like the most unusual place to live. Long ago, ancient empires and civilizations left behind **ruins**. Throughout Europe, in countries like Italy or Greece, there are many destroyed buildings and cities. But ruins can be found in the United States, too. Across the southwestern United States there are ruins of ancient cities. Unlike most cities, these were built in big caves high up in the **cliffs**. Who lived in them? Why were they in cliffs?

2   Like many historical mysteries, we have to go way back in time to find the answer. For hundreds or even thousands of years, Native Americans lived in the Southwest. They grew corn, beans, squash, and melons. They built their homes near their fields. Back then, there was a lot of rain, so crops were very plentiful. More and more people came to share the wealth and as a result, the **villages** became larger.

3   But after a while, **tribes** from farther north began raiding these peaceful villages. The villagers protected themselves by building their homes in caves at the top of nearby cliffs. It was a matter of survival. The Native Americans constructed their cliff dwellings out of rock. Most buildings were two or three stories high. The cliff dwellers used **ladders** to reach entrances on the roofs. In case of attack, the ladders could be pulled up. Up to 1,500 people could live in one of these cities.

4   Eventually, the cliff dwellers left the caves. In 1100 A.D., the rains stopped. There wasn't enough water so they had to look for a new place to live. Historians believe that the cliff dwellers most likely moved farther south to find better farmland. Or perhaps increasing enemy attacks made them leave. Whatever the reason, the cliff dwellings were abandoned long before the first white settlers came to America.

## Vocabulary Study

**A  Choose and write the correct word.**

| ruins    cliffs    villages    tribes    ladders |

1.  There are many different ____________ in South Africa.

2.  Roger loves to climb ____________ for fun.

3.  The ____________ in Rome give you insight into history.

4.  Firefighters use ____________ for tall buildings.

5.  The small ____________ in France were charming.

**B  Replace the underlined words with a synonym from the box.**

| wealth    raiding    stories    enemy    dwellings |

1.  Their <u>homes</u> were large and comfortable.

2.  The skyscraper has 51 <u>floors</u>.

3.  The pirates shared the <u>bounty</u> with each other.

4.  A long time ago, the English were the French's <u>adversary</u>.

5.  The people started <u>attacking</u> the town.

## Main idea

This story is about ______________.
 a.  caves and cliffs    b.  tribes who were violent
 c.  people who lived in cliffs  d.  rain and crops

## Paragraph Understanding

Choose the correct answer.

1. Paragraph ____    There are ruins in southwestern United States.
2. Paragraph ____    Native Americans built cities in caves.
3. Paragraph ____    Native Americans lived near crop fields.
4. Paragraph ____    The cliff dwellers left the caves and moved south.

## Looking for detail

Circle the correct answer.

1. Native Americans in the Southwest grew ____________.
   - a. squash
   - b. potatoes
   - c. apples
   - d. pumpkins

2. The cliff dwellings' doors were ___________.
   - a. hidden
   - b. on the roofs
   - c. locked
   - d. sealed shut

3. Which paragraph talks about there not being enough water?
   - a. Paragraph 1
   - b. Paragraph 2
   - c. Paragraph 3
   - d. Paragraph 4

4. After the people moved to the cliffs the enemies were probably ___________.
   - a. very happy
   - b. less successful at raiding
   - c. upset and moved away
   - d. better at attacking them

## Developing Skills

**Find a grammatical mistake and correct it.**

1. Ruins can be found in the United States to.

   _______________________________________________

2. The cities were built in big caves high on in cliffs.

   _______________________________________________

3. There was a lot of rains then.

   _______________________________________________

4. The ladders could be pull up.

   _______________________________________________

5. The Native Americans grew beans and corns.

   _______________________________________________

### T 40　Summary & Listening Practice

**Read the paragraph and fill in as many blanks as you can.**
**Then listen to the recording and fill in the rest of the blanks.**

America has ① _____________ of ancient cities, too. The cities were in big caves high up in ② _____________. Native Americans used to grow crops in fields in the Southwest. There was a lot of rain then, so the crops grew well. ③ _____________ from the north started to attack their villages. So, they moved to the cliffs. The cliff ④ _____________ were very big. About 1,500 people could live in one of the cities. When the rains stopped, the cliff dwellers ⑤ _____________ the cities.

# BuildUp Reading

Developing Advanced Reading Skills

## Workbook

Level 1

WorldCom ELT

# Sleep Tight, Everyone!

## Vocabulary & Idioms

**exhausted** — *adj.* very tired
Ex. *She was exhausted from the day's work.*

**battery** — *n.* a source of energy, usually a cell used to produce electricity
Ex. *Are there batteries in the camera?*

**ideal** — *adj.* perfect
Ex. *He has found his ideal job.*

**brain** — *n.* an organ in the head that acts as the control center of the body and is capable of producing thoughts
Ex. *The brain of a human is much larger than that of a dog.*

**curious** — *adj.* eager to know, having many questions
Ex. *I was very curious about how he was able to do that.*

**rapid** — *adj.* very quick
Ex. *The rapid movement of the river's water can be dangerous.*

**discover** — *v.* to find
Ex. *He discovered that the milk had gone bad.*

**midst** — *n.* middle
Ex. *I was in the midst of doing work when someone telephoned.*

**vivid** — *adj.* full of life
Ex. *I can't stop looking at this vivid painting.*

**crucial** — *adj.* required, needed
Ex. *It is crucial for animals to learn how to survive at an early age.*

**necessary** — *adj.* required, crucial
Ex. *For most people, eight hours of sleep is necessary per night.*

**function** — *v.* to work, operate
Ex. *Is the TV functioning properly?*

## A Choose the best word(s) to fill in the blank.

1. The CD player is not working because there are no ____________.

   a. brains      b. batteries      c. drums      d. money

2. I was caught in the ____________ of the storm.

   a. tree      b. back      c. midst      d. weight

3. His ____________ speech was hard to understand.

   a. rapid      b. ideal      c. necessary      d. crucial

4. I ____________ a hole in the wall.

   a. functioned      b. discovered      c. ate      d. watched

5. The tiring job left her ____________.

   a. vivid      b. crucial      c. necessary      d. exhausted

## B Choose the correct form of the word to fill in the blanks.

1. There could ____________ a problem.

   a. is      b. was      c. be

2. He needs at least eight hours of ____________.

   a. sleep      b. sleeps      c. slept

3. I hope that I can ____________ today at work.

   a. will function      b. function      c. functioned

4. This is the ____________ job for me.

   a. ideal      b. idea      c. ideally

5. It is not ____________ to do that.

   a. necessarily      b. necessary      c. necessitate

## Listening  T41

**Listen to the lecture and choose the best answer.**

1. What is the lecture mainly about?
   a. Sleeping habits
   b. The nervous system
   c. REM sleep
   d. newborn babies

2. What is true about the purpose of REM sleep?
   a. It has been confirmed.
   b. It is to relax our bodies.
   c. We're not sure about it.
   d. It is to rest our minds.

3 Lack of REM sleep might lead to ___________ .
   a. cancer       b. depression       c. diabetes       d. leukemia

## Grammar Review

**Choose the correct one.**

1. Experts advise us ___________ out regularly.
   [work/ to work/ working]

2. Medical scientists have ___________ to find a cure for cancer.
   [trying/ was trying/ been trying]

3. We do not know how ___________ for the new project.
   [much is needed/ is much needed/ needed is much]

4. Helen Keller ___________ June 27, 1880.
   [born was in/ was born on/ has been born on]

5. Nobody understood ___________ .
   [he said what/ what did he say/ what he said]

## Vocabulary & Idioms

**fluid**
*adj.* readily changeable, not fixed
*Ex.* *The athlete's movements are very fluid.*

**childhood**
*n.* the time spent as a child
*Ex.* *Many of my childhood memories are still vivid.*

**affectionately**
*adv.* with love
*Ex.* *His wife treats him affectionately.*

**nickname**
*n.* a name used in place of a real or proper name
*Ex.* *Because she is such a fast runner, her nickname is Jet.*

**circulate**
*v.* to go around
*Ex.* *The newspaper circulated throughout the town.*

**of course**
certainly, definitely
*Ex.* *Of course, I cannot jump that high.*

**come up with**
to think of first
*Ex.* *I came up with that idea.*

**compound**
*adj.* having two or more parts
*Ex.* *These compound leaves have more than one lobe.*

**mechanical**
*adj.* relating to machines
*Ex.* *These mechanical objects need to be fixed.*

**flexible**
*adj.* bendable, changeable, accommodating
*Ex.* *My schedule is very flexible.*

**pop culture**
popular music, movies, books, etc. of a culture
*Ex.* *Pop culture often influences the behavior of young kids.*

**in context**
in the particular set of words or phrases that we say at a certain time describing a particular event, situation, etc.
*Ex.* *In context, the words that he said to his friend do not sound as bad.*

## Vocabulary Review

**A  Choose the best word(s) to fill in the blank.**

1. Salt is an example of a ____________ substance.
   a. compound        b. mechanical      c. vivid            d. rapid

2. ____________, you can do it.
   a. In context        b. Lately            c. Of course        d. Ideally

3. Who ____________ that phrase?
   a. came up with     b. saw              c. became           d. watched

4. His ____________ is Fat Sam.
   a. nickname         b. childhood        c. toy              d. sweater

5. What do those words mean ____________?
   a. affectionately    b. highly            c. freely            d. in context

**B  Choose the correct form of the word to fill in the blanks.**

1. They hugged ____________.
   a. affectionate                  b. affection                  c. affectionately

2. The material is very ____________.
   a. flex                          b. flexible                   c. flexibility

3. Who ____________ that awful rumor?
   a. circulating                   b. circulated                 c. circle

4. I spent a lot of time reading during my ____________.
   a. childhood                     b. children                   c. child

5. Today's ____________ features many musical artists.
   a. population culture            b. pop culture                c. culture pop

## Listening  T 42

### Listen to the lecture and choose the best answer.

1. What is the lecture mainly about?
   a. World geography
   b. Dialects
   c. The wide use of English and its many forms
   d. US and Great Britain relations

2. Which country does NOT use English as an official language?
   a. Canada                      b. The Philippines
   c. South Africa                d. Mexico

3. What is true about English?
   a. English has many accents and dialects.
   b. British English sounds the same as American English.
   c. About fifty countries use English as an official language.
   d. A southern accent refers to a South African accent.

## Grammar Review

### Choose the correct one.

1. One of the _____________ in life is health.
   [important most things/ things important most/ most important things]

2. William Strunk's book _____________ the "little book."
   [known as was/ was known as/ as was known]

3. The company decided _____________ completely different products.
   [to begin making/ making to begin/ begin to making]

4. We need to thank _____________ their lives to defend our country.
   [who those sacrificed/ those who sacrificed/ who sacrificed those]

5. _____________ hard, Maria passed the entrance examination.
   [Studying by really/ Really studying by/ By studying really]

## Vocabulary & Idioms

**gifted**    *adj.*   talented
*Ex.*   *He is a very gifted athlete.*

**soloist**    *n.*   one who performs a musical composition or part of a musical composition that is written to be performed by one singer or instrumentalist
*Ex.*   *The piano soloist stood up for applause.*

**under pressure**    during times of urgency
*Ex.*   *The secretary works well under pressure.*

**piece**    *n.*   a musical composition
*Ex.*   *This piece was written by Mozart.*

**gasp**    *v.*   to breathe suddenly because you are shocked
*Ex.*   *He gasped at the sight.*

**grace**    *n.*   elegance or beauty of form, manner, or movement
*Ex.*   *She demonstrated much grace in her dance.*

**effortlessly**    *adv.*   easily
*Ex.*   *I finished the project effortlessly.*

**conductor**    *n.*   a person who directs a chorus or orchestra
*Ex.*   *He is the conductor of a grand orchestra.*

**applaud**    *v.*   to clap the hands to express approval
*Ex.*   *The audience applauded the performance.*

**front page**    *n.*   the cover of a newspaper or magazine
*Ex.*   *The famous actor's picture appeared on the front page.*

**local**    *adj.*   relating to a particular area or location
*Ex.*   *We should visit the local store.*

**poise**    *n.*   composure, a state of dignified or self-confident manner
*Ex.*   *It is important to show poise on stage.*

**A  Choose the best word(s) to fill in the blank.**

1. The actor is performing ____________.
   a. formerly          b. aback          c. out loud          d. under pressure

2. It is hard to maintain ____________ when everything seems to be going wrong.
   a. poise          b. intelligence     c. courage          d. anger

3. The ____________ musician learned very quickly.
   a. mechanical     b. gifted          c. soloist          d. clumsy

4. The ____________ moved his arms rapidly while directing the orchestra.
   a. conductor      b. soloist          c. secretary          d. president

5. The ____________ bus station is just around the corner.
   a. gifted          b. fluid          c. local          d. faraway

**B  Choose the correct form of the word to fill in the blanks.**

1. The president made the speech ____________.
   a. effortlessly          b. effortless          c. effort

2. It is customary to ____________ after a performance.
   a. applauding          b. applauded          c. applaud

3. When will you ____________ to the post office?
   a. went          b. go          c. going

4. The ____________ in which she walked made her stand out.
   a. grace          b. graceful          c. gracefully

5. When he saw how large the building was, he ____________.
   a. gasp          b. gasped          c. gasping

## Listening  T43

### Listen to the lecture and choose the best answer.

1. What is the lecture mainly about?
   a. The creation of Partners in Performance
   b. The Avery Fisher Prize
   c. The life of Midori
   d. New York University

2. Where was Midori born?
   a. Osaka, Japan
   b. New York
   c. Tokyo, Japan
   d. Beijing, China

3. What is true of Midori?
   a. She moved to New York with her father.
   b. She learned to play the violin by herself.
   c. She started several organizations with her prize money.
   d. She attended Columbia University.

## Grammar Review

### Choose the correct one.

1. When she was five years old, Michelle ____________ Chinese.
   [learn to began/ to learn began/ began to learn]

2. A renowned scholar ____________ give a speech to the students.
   [invited was to/ was invited to/ to invited was]

3. Brian told us about the accident as if ____________ it himself.
   [he had seen/ had he seen/ seen he had]

4. There was ____________ for us to discuss.
   [important issue another/ issue  important/ another important issue]

5. Despite all the fuss, ____________.
   [remained Jenny calm/ Jenny remained calm/ Jenny calm remained]

# chew, chew, chewing gum

## Vocabulary & Idioms

| | | |
|---|---|---|
| **convenience store** | | a store that has a few selection of items but is open long hours |
| | *Ex.* | *7-Eleven is an example of a convenience store.* |
| **disgusting** | *adj.* | filling with distaste, exciting nausea |
| | *Ex.* | *I find that combination of ingredients very disgusting.* |
| **date back** | | started |
| | *Ex.* | *The creation of this machine dates back to the 1920s.* |
| **take for granted** | | to accept in a careless or indifferent manner |
| | *Ex.* | *The availability of food in some countries today is taken for granted.* |
| **prize** | *v.* | to value |
| | *Ex.* | *This prized food is difficult to find.* |
| **fluid** | *n.* | liquid |
| | *Ex.* | *He poured the fluid out of the jar.* |
| **bark** | *n.* | the outer covering of a tree trunk |
| | *Ex.* | *The inner bark of the cinnamon tree has a unique smell.* |
| **gummy** | *adj.* | sticky like gum |
| | *Ex.* | *The gummy substance stuck to the wall.* |
| **ingredient** | *n.* | an element of a mixture |
| | *Ex.* | *Milk is one of the main ingredients in ice cream.* |
| **export** | *v.* | to send to another country for sale |
| | *Ex.* | *Our company exports cars to the United States.* |
| **artificial** | *adj.* | not of nature |
| | *Ex.* | *These flowers are artificial and made of plastic.* |
| **popular** | *adj.* | well liked |
| | *Ex.* | *The mayor is very popular among the citizens of New York.* |

## Vocabulary Review

**A  Choose the best word(s) to fill in the blank.**

1. This flavor of ice cream is ____________.
   a. liberal          b. artificial          c. fluid                    d. violent

2. What are the ____________ for making meatloaf?
   a. ingredients    b. componets    c. times                    d. hypotheses

3. The importance of this device should not be ____________.
   a. popular          b. exported          c. taken for granted      d. prized

4. The start of the war ____________ to half a century ago.
   a. dates back    b. ended          c. looked                    d. celebrated

5. I cannot eat any more of this ____________ food.
   a. exported      b. disgusting      c. artificial                d. fluid

**B  Choose the correct form of the word to fill in the blanks.**

1. The people have ____________ this location because of its wonderful scenery.
   a. prizing                b. prize                    c. prized

2. I will ____________ these products to China.
   a. export                b. exported                c. exporting

3. He ____________ walking to the convenience store.
   a. will                    b. be                        c. is

4. Everyone is drinking the ____________ drink.
   a. popularity            b. popular                c. populate

5. The ____________ sells many items.
   a. convenience store    b. convenient store    c. convenience stores

### Listen to the lecture and choose the best answer.

1. What is the lecture mainly about?
   a. Smokers and users of tobacco
   b. Different types of gum and their uses
   c. Teeth cleaning
   d. Different flavors of gum

2. What is true about gum?
   a. Gum can be used to repair skin.
   b. Gum is unpopular.
   c. Some gum contain nicotine.
   d. Gum is dangerously unhealthy.

3. Which of the following types of gum was NOT mentioned in the lecture?
   a. Icebreakers
   b. Trident
   c. Nicorette
   d. Doublemint

## Grammar Review

### Choose the correct one.

1. _____________ think of Monica's performance?
   [What do you / How do you / What you do]

2. Too many people _____________ that they are healthy.
   [it take for granted / granted it take / take it for granted]

3. That is the _____________ I've ever seen.
   [most movie amazing / most amazing movie / amazing most movie]

4. _____________ gathered at the rally.
   [Of thousands people / Of people thousands / Thousands of people]

5. If I were you, I _____________ Norway.
   [would to travel / would travel to / travel to would]

## Vocabulary & Idioms

| | | |
|---|---|---|
| **aspiring** | *adj.* | having great ambition |
| | *Ex.* | *The aspiring businessman eventually rose to great wealth and fame.* |
| **publisher** | *n.* | a person or company that prints and issues books, newspapers, magazines, etc. |
| | *Ex.* | *The publisher issued four new books last week.* |
| **cartoon** | *n.* | a drawing showing a funny situation |
| | *Ex.* | *This cartoon always makes me laugh.* |
| **edition** | *n.* | one of a series of a book, newspaper, magazine, etc. |
| | *Ex.* | *Have you read the new edition of Popular Science magazine yet?* |
| **peculiar** | *adj.* | odd, unusual |
| | *Ex.* | *She looked very peculiar today with her strange looking outfit.* |
| **bald** | *adj.* | having no hair |
| | *Ex.* | *My grandfather is bald.* |
| **barefoot** | *adj.* | without shoes or socks |
| | *Ex.* | *He would rather walk around barefoot than wear shoes.* |
| **nightshirt** | *n.* | a shirt worn at night to sleep in |
| | *Ex.* | *The boy's dark colored nightshirt made him hard to see at night.* |
| **hire** | *v.* | to engage the services of a person for wages or other payment |
| | *Ex.* | *I hired two boys to help me paint my house.* |
| **style** | *n.* | way of expressing thought |
| | *Ex.* | *His style of writing is very direct and concise.* |
| **successive** | *adj.* | following in order |
| | *Ex.* | *The band marched in a successive fashion.* |
| **comic** | *n.* | a drawing or sequence of drawings that tell a funny story |
| | *Ex.* | *Ben is the artist of this comic.* |

**A Choose the best word(s) to fill in the blank.**

1. This is the second ___________ of the book.
   a. publisher     b. edition     c. comic     d. title

2. Jenny is sleeping in a ___________.
   a. nightshirt     b. sock     c. sandal     d. boot

3. Bob has a unique ___________ of playing the instrument.
   a. part     b. section     c. piece     d. style

4. Who is the ___________ of this magazine?
   a. edition     b. cartoon     c. comic     d. publisher

5. His jacket looks so ___________.
   a. peculiar     b. aspiring     c. bald     d. barefoot

**B Choose the correct form of the word to fill in the blanks.**

1. The manager ___________ new employees for the job.
   a. hired     b. hiring     c. hire

2. The ___________ young politician works hard every day.
   a. aspire     b. aspiring     c. aspired

3. I wanted to ___________ the vehicle.
   a. used     b. use     c. using

4. His ___________ head was very shiny.
   a. bald     b. balding     c. baldness

5. This is one of my favorite ___________.
   a. comics     b. comical     c. comicality

## Listening  T45

**Listen to the lecture and choose the best answer.**

1. What is the lecture mainly about?
   a. Yellow journalism and its consequences
   b. The New York World and its history
   c. The New York Journal  and its history
   d. The Spanish-American War

2. Would is NOT part of yellow journalism?
   a. Information about scandals
   b. controversial topics
   c. propaganda
   d. accurate weather reports

3. What is true about yellow journalism?
   a. It started in Europe.
   b. It started in America.
   c. It was honest journalism.
   d. It was beneficial.

## Grammar Review

**Choose the correct one.**

1. Actually, there are ____________ improve your performance.
   [ways to many/ ways many to/ many ways to]

2. ____________ girl, Anna did not like speaking with strangers.
   [Being a shy/ Shy being a/ A being shy]

3. ____________ was strict, Tom let his son have a choice.
   [Even he though/ He even though/ Even though he]

4. Bill ____________ many different things in his own words.
   [writing kept about/ kept writing about/ about writing kept]

5. World War II ____________ 1939.
   [out broke in/ broke out on/ broke out in]

## Vocabulary & Idioms

**equally**  
*adv.* to the same degree  
*Ex.* The pie was divided equally.

**struggle**  
*v.* to fight a problem resolutely, strive  
*Ex.* Martin Luther King struggled for African American rights.

**belong**  
*v.* to be suitable  
*Ex.* Do you think that animals belong outside?

**sensible**  
*adj.* having good sense or sound judgment  
*Ex.* We need sensible people here at our company.

**discuss**  
*v.* to talk over, to consider or examine by argument  
*Ex.* Can we discuss this later?

**matter**  
*n.* situation, state, business  
*Ex.* What is the matter?

**declare**  
*v.* to make known or state clearly  
*Ex.* I declare that this story is true.

**duty**  
*n.* something that one is required to do  
*Ex.* His duty is to clean the floors after every class.

**tax**  
*n.* money paid to the government for its services  
*Ex.* The government is planning to raise taxes this year.

**gradually**  
*adv.* slowly advancing  
*Ex.* The tree grew gradually every day.

**territory**  
*n.* a tract of land, district  
*Ex.* This territory is controlled by the United States.

**election**  
*n.* the choosing of a person or persons for office by vote  
*Ex.* The presidential election is next week.

## Vocabulary Review

**A  Choose the best word(s) to fill in the blank.**

1. Has the judge ______________ the winner yet?
   a. struggled       b. structured       c. wrestled       d. declared

2. Eudcation is a serious ______________ .
   a. territory       b. matter       c. duty       d. edition

3. It is my ______________ to protect you.
   a. border       b. simplicity       c. duty       d. ease

4. The next ______________ for mayor is in May.
   a. edition       b. election       c. period       d. occasion

5. He is a[n] ______________ man of good judgement.
   a. sensible       b. barefoot       c. weak       d. artificial

**B  Choose the correct form of the word to fill in the blanks.**

1. This morning, I ______________ to make it to work on time.
   a. struggler              b. struggled              c. struggling

2. This car ______________ to me.
   a. belonging              b. belongs              c. belong

3. Through practice, I ______________ became a better soccer player.
   a. gradual              b. graduate              c. gradually

4. Have you ______________ it with your parents yet?
   a. discussed              b. discussion              c. discussing

5. Please divide the pizza ______________ .
   a. equally              b. equalized              c. equality

## Listen to the lecture and choose the best answer.

1. What is the lecture mainly about?
   a. Women's suffrage
   b. Cultural differences
   c. Abortion
   d. A brief history of feminism

2. What is true about feminism?
   a. The first wave started in the 1700s.
   b. Women argued for equality in the workplace.
   c. The first wave occurred in the United States and Germany.
   d. The second wave and first wave of feminism continue to coexist today.

3. Which of the following was NOT a wave of feminism mentioned in the lecture?
   a. Women's right to go into space
   b. Women's suffrage
   c. Redefining feminism
   d. Sexual discrimination

## Grammar Review

### Choose the correct one.

1. As an adult, you should learn ___________ your own mistakes.
   [laugh to at / at laugh to / to laugh at]

2. ___________ world, Erica enjoyed meeting new people.
   [Around traveling the / Traveling around the / The traveling around]

3. An innovative product ___________ an imaginative scientist.
   [was invented by / invented was by / by invented was]

4. We make mistakes, learn lessons, ___________.
   [and growing up / and grown up / and grow up]

5. Susan's father let ___________ at the party.
   [fun her have / her have fun / have her fun]

## Vocabulary & Idioms

**mind**    *n.*    the ability to think and reason
*Ex.*   *Have you lost your mind?*

**figure out**    to understand, to solve
*Ex.*   *After hours of working, Sam finally figured out the problem.*

**risk**    *v.*    to expose oneself to chances of loss or injury
*Ex.*   *I risked my job to help you.*

**village**    *n.*    a small town
*Ex.*   *The village has a population of 300 people.*

**temple**    *n.*    a building of worship for a god or gods
*Ex.*   *The monks are praying at the temple.*

**statue**    *n.*    a three dimensional work of art
*Ex.*   *This statue of the king was over two stories high.*

**sail**    *v.*    to travel by water aboard a ship, boat, raft, etc.
*Ex.*   *A couple centuries ago, the first pilgrims sailed to America.*

**raft**    *n.*    a flat structure that floats on water used for transport
*Ex.*   *We made a sturdy raft from logs and planks.*

**impossible**    *adj.*    not capable of occurring or happening
*Ex.*   *Is it impossible to fly to Mars?*

**theory**    *n.*    a proposed explanation for something
*Ex.*   *Do you have any theories about how it could have happened?*

**modern**    *adj.*    relating to the present time
*Ex.*   *Modern equipment is much more advanced than equipment of the past.*

**encounter**    *v.*    to meet with unexpectedly
*Ex.*   *As the thief ran out of the store, he encountered two policemen waiting for him.*

**A** Choose the best word(s) to fill in the blank.

1. My _____________ is filled with thoughts at the moment.
   a. hand　　　　　b. eyes　　　　　c. raft　　　　　d. mind

2. The _____________ of George Washington looks almost exactly like him!
   a. statue　　　　b. temple　　　　c. territory　　　　d. raft

3. I find it _____________ to finish all this work by tomorrow.
   a. modern　　　　b. impossible　　　c. peculiar　　　　d. gifted

4. Did you hear that Billy _____________ a shark in the ocean yesterday?
   a. risked　　　　b. sailed　　　　c. encountered　　　d. struggled

5. I live in a small _____________.
   a. printing　　　b. village　　　　c. statue　　　　d. edition

**B** Choose the correct form of the word to fill in the blanks.

1. Have you ever _____________ your life to do something?
   a. risk　　　　　b. risky　　　　　c. risked

2. We are lucky to live in a _____________ society.
   a. modernize　　b. modernization　　c. modern

3. My _____________ is that this was all done by the dog.
   a. theorizing　　b. theoretical　　c. theory

4. I can't _____________ out this problem!
   a. figured　　　b. figure　　　　c. figuring

5. _____________ across the Atlantic Ocean in a raft would be quite difficult
   and dangerous.
   a. Sailing　　　b. Sailor　　　　c. Sail

**Listening**  T47

### Listen to the lecture and choose the best answer.

1. What is the lecture mainly about?
   a. The first settlers of Polynesian Islands
   b. Easter Island's vast landscape
   c. The Native Americans' arrival to Easter Island
   d. An old Incan legend

2. What is true about Easter Island?
   a. It was inhabited by Incans.
   b. The natives have handed down oral history.
   c. Southwestern Native Americans settled there.
   d. Heyerdahl discovered Easter Island.

3. Which of the following does NOT support Heyerdahl's theory?
   a. An old Incan Legend
   b. Eastern Island oral history
   c. Jakob Roggeveen's discovery
   d. Peru oral history

## Grammar Review

### Choose the correct one.

1. Helen Keller is ____________ a great thinker.
   [as thought of / thought of as / of thought as]

2. The price of the car was ____________ only the rich could afford to buy it.
   [high that so / so that high / so high that]

3. Before he came to Korea, Peter ____________ England.
   [had lived in / lived had in / in had lived]

4. It would ____________ write so many pages within a day.
   [impossible to be / to be impossible / be impossible to]

5. They ____________ up with that idea.
   [could come have / could have come / have come could]

## Vocabulary & Idioms

| | | |
|---|---|---|
| **passion** | *n.* | a powerful feeling of love or hate |
| | *Ex.* | *The couple shows their passion by embracing each other.* |
| **medical school** | | school for those wishing to be a doctor, surgeon, etc. |
| | *Ex.* | *After graduating from the university, Eddie went on to attend medical school.* |
| **pursue** | *v.* | to follow |
| | *Ex.* | *The police pursed the criminal down the street.* |
| **determined** | *adj.* | resolute, decided |
| | *Ex.* | *I am determined to finish the race.* |
| **laboratory** | *n.* | a place for conducting scientific research |
| | *Ex.* | *The laboratory is for employees only.* |
| **fascinate** | *v.* | to attract and hold attentively by a unique power |
| | *Ex.* | *The boy was fascinated at the sight of so many stars in the night sky.* |
| **cell** | *n.* | the smallest living unit of an organism |
| | *Ex.* | *Scientists are interested in how cells grow and divide.* |
| **microscope** | *n.* | a device used to see very tiny objects |
| | *Ex.* | *In order to see the bacteria, you must use a microscope.* |
| **succeed** | *v.* | to accomplish |
| | *Ex.* | *Did you succeed in cooking a nice meal?* |
| **threaten** | *v.* | to be a danger to |
| | *Ex.* | *The hurricane threatened the safety of the houses.* |
| **entire** | *adj.* | all of |
| | *Ex.* | *Did you eat the entire pizza by yourself?* |
| **chemical** | *n.* | a material produced by a reaction involving atoms and molecules |
| | *Ex.* | *The factory releases harmful chemicals into the air.* |

## Vocabulary Review

### A Choose the best word(s) to fill in the blank.

1. If you want to be a doctor, when are you planning to attend ___________?
   a. the laboratory    b. medical school    c. the village    d. the temple

2. Do you have a ___________ for soccer?
   a. passion          b. theory          c. temple          d. statue

3. A ___________ is a tool for observing things.
   a. laboratory        b. village          c. microscope    d. temple

4. Billy is ___________ to accomplish the task.
   a. determined        b. fascinated        c. threatened    d. pursued

5. The ___________ room was staring at him.
   a. entire            b. impossible        c. modern          d. sensible

### B Choose the correct form of the word to fill in the blanks.

1. How long are you going to ___________ this dream?
   a. pursue            b. pursuit          c. pursuing

2. Have you ___________ in writing your first book?
   a. success          b. succeeded        c. succession

3. The mountains look ___________.
   a. threaten          b. threatening      c. threat

4. Some ___________ can be very bad for your health.
   a. chemicals        b. chemic          c. chemistry

5. I'm studying this plant ___________ under the microscope.
   a. cellular          b. cellulite        c. cell

**Listen to the lecture and choose the best answer.**

1.  What is the lecture mainly about?
    a. Sweden during World War II      b. European concentration camps
    c. The Holocaust      d. Jewish culture and religion

2.  What is true about Jews during World War II?
    a. Jews had a very easy time.
    b. Jewish culture flourished.
    c. Jews migrated to Russia.
    d. Many Jews died in concentration camps.

3.  Which country did many Jews escape to during World War II?
    a. Sweden      b. Canada
    c. Russia      d. Greece

## Grammar Review

**Choose the correct one.**

1.  All the teachers wanted the student ____________ lawyer.
    [be to a/ to be a/ a be to]

2.  Suprisingly, Adam ____________ cross the river by swimming.
    [able to was/ was to able/ was able to]

3.  I think ____________ disagree with you, but you need to be strong.
    [other person may/ other people may/ another people may]

4.  The incident led many ____________ about better ways to protect the environment.
    [to think people/ think to people/ people to think]

5.  The material is widely ____________ a variety of eco-friendly products.
    [used to make/ make to used/ to make used]

# Susan Cervantes:
## The Wall Painter



## Vocabulary & Idioms

| | | |
|---|---|---|
| **traditionally** | *adv.* | relating to time-honored doctrines or customs |
| | *Ex.* | *Americans traditionally eat turkey for Thanksgiving Day.* |
| **canvas** | *n.* | a piece of heavily woven cloth |
| | *Ex.* | *The painter bought three new canvases for his next project.* |
| **life-sized** | *adj.* | of natural or original size of a person, object, etc. |
| | *Ex.* | *Is this statue of a bull life-sized?* |
| **mural** | *n.* | a painting on a wall |
| | *Ex.* | *The mural on the side of the building is very famous.* |
| **lively** | *adj.* | full of life, energetic |
| | *Ex.* | *Salsa is a lively dance.* |
| **blank** | *adj.* | empty |
| | *Ex.* | *Why do you have such a blank expression on your face?* |
| **liven up** | | to brighten, to put life into |
| | *Ex.* | *The paintings on the wall livened up our living room.* |
| **decorate** | *v.* | to make something look nice or pleasing |
| | *Ex.* | *How do you plan to decorate your room?* |
| **reflect** | *v.* | to make apparent or visible |
| | *Ex.* | *His hard work reflects his determination to succeed.* |
| **aspect** | *n.* | characteristic, trait |
| | *Ex.* | *His kindness is a good aspect of his personality.* |
| **gang** | *n.* | a close group of young people that commonly engage in delinquent behavior |
| | *Ex.* | *The gang of teenagers roamed the streets.* |
| **custom** | *n.* | a habitual practice |
| | *Ex.* | *In Asia, it is a custom to take off your shoes before entering someone's home.* |

**A  Choose the best word(s) to fill in the blank.**

1. The artist is painting on a ___________.
   a. canvas          b. cell          c. laboratory          d. statue

2. Are you familiar with the ___________ of Russians?
   a. customs          b. canvas          c. laboratory          d. murals

3. It was ___________ believed that the Earth was flat.
   a. lively          b. gradually          c. eventually          d. traditionally

4. How long did it take to paint that giant ___________ on the wall?
   a. mural          b. microscope          c. laboratory          d. temple

5. The party was very ___________.
   a. life-sized          b. impossible          c. lively          d. blank

**B  Choose the correct form of the word to fill in the blanks.**

1. Have you ever ___________ a Christmas tree before?
   a. decoration          b. decorated          c. decorating

2. Where ___________ you going tomorrow?
   a. will be          b. was          c. are

3. I've never seen anyone ___________ so well.
   a. sing          b. sang          c. to sing

4. I ___________ to school tomorrow.
   a. walked          b. to walk          c. will walk

5. Sarah is ___________ a sad movie.
   a. watch          b. watching          c. watched

## Listening  T49

### Listen to the lecture and choose the best answer.

1. What is the lecture mainly about?
   a. Graffiti art
   b. New York City vandalism
   c. The Metropolitan Transit Authority
   d. Hip-hop culture

2. What is true about graffiti?
   a. Graffiti is popular with the police.
   b. Graffiti art uses oil paint.
   c. Graffiti is a part of rock & roll culture.
   d. Graffiti art can be very large and elaborate.

3. Who began efforts to remove graffiti?
   a. Susan Cervantes
   b. The Metropolitan Transit Authority
   c. New York City gangsters
   d. Local hip-hop artists

## Grammar Review

### Choose the correct one.

1. That is a ____________ fish.
   [kind rare of/ rare kind of/ of kind rare]

2. There ____________ an old temple on the hill.
   [used to be/ to used be/ be used to]

3. That was the most ____________ ever seen.
   [film boring I'd/ I'd film boring/ boring film I'd]

4. Although his parents were poor, Kevin was ____________.
   [them of proud/ proud of them/ proud in them]

5. His advisor told ____________ from alcohol.
   [to abstain him/ him abstain to/ him to abstain]

# 10 COLOR BLINDNESS



**organ**  *n.*  a group of tissues that perform a function in the body, such as the heart, kidney, etc.

*Ex.*  *Take care of yourself or you may one day need an organ transplant.*

**sensitive**  *adj.*  readily affected by outside stimuli or influences

*Ex.*  *Her skin seemed very sensitive to touch.*

**glasses**  *n.*  a pair of lenses on a light frame that is used to correct vision

*Ex.*  *I bought a new pair of glasses.*

**unfortunately**  *adv.*  by bad luck

*Ex.*  *He was unfortunately injured in the situation.*

**correct**  *v.*  to fix, remove the errors, set right or make true

*Ex.*  *I corrected my mistake.*

**blindness**  *n.*  the inability to see

*Ex.*  *The darkness of the room caused temporary blindness.*

**misleading**  *adj.*  deceptive, tricky

*Ex.*  *Fred's unfriendly appearance is misleading.*

**originate from**  to come from, to have started from

*Ex.*  *Kim-chee originates from Korea.*

**common**  *adj.*  appearing or occurring often, widespread

*Ex.*  *That sign is very common.*

**shade**  *n.*  the degree of darkness of a color

*Ex.*  *The tree leaves are a darker shade of green than the grass.*

**typically**  *adv.*  usually

*Ex.*  *I typically go to bed at around 11 pm.*

**inherit**  *v.*  to receive from parents through heredity

*Ex.*  *I inherited blue eyes from my mother.*

## Vocabulary Review

**A  Choose the best word(s) to fill in the blank.**

1. ____________, I could not do anything to stop the disaster.
   a. Fortunately     b. Unknowingly     c. Unfortunately     d. Lately

2. Please ____________ your wrong answers.
   a. correct          b. inherit          c. attend          d. compose

3. How many ____________ of blue paint does the store have?
   a. customs          b. shades          c. aspects          d. traits

4. Who did you ____________ your beautiful blond hair from?
   a. correct          b. reflect          c. threaten          d. inherit

5. I need ____________ to read.
   a. glasses          b. organs          c. customs          d. murals

**B  Choose the correct form of the word to fill in the blanks.**

1. What are you ____________ here?
   a. do                      b. did                      c. doing

2. Where can I go ____________ new shoes?
   a. get                     b. to get                  c. got

3. The city is ____________ fairly cold.
   a. typically              b. type                    c. typical

4. The title of the book is quite ____________.
   a. misled                 b. misleading              c. mislead

5. A few minutes ago, we ____________ an eagle fly past.
   a. see                     b. saw                     c. will see

**Listen to the lecture and choose the best answer.**

1. What is the lecture mainly about?
   a. Sea mammals
   b. Mammals
   c. Color blindness in animals
   d. Primates

2. What is true about mammals?
   a. They are mostly dichromats.
   b. They are usually cold-blooded.
   c. They are mostly trichromats
   d. Humans are not mammals.

3. Which of the following is NOT a dichromat?
   a. Dogs
   b. Cats
   c. Mice
   d. Sharks

**Grammar Review**

**Choose the correct one.**

1. You _____________ Carpenters. I've heard a lot about you.
   [must Susan be/ must be Susan/ can't be Susan]

2. This is a _____________ Mariah Carey was born.
   [in village which/ which village in/ village in which]

3. Many theories of language _____________.
   [can be misleads/ can be misleading/ can be mislead]

4. Unfortunately, the machine did _____________.
   [work perfectly not/ perfectly work not/ not work perfectly]

5. There _____________ kinds of people in our society.
   [are many different/ different many are/ many are different]

## Vocabulary & Idioms

| | | |
|---|---|---|
| **delight** | *v.* | to give great pleasure |
| | *Ex.* | *It always delights me to eat good food.* |
| **rare** | *adj.* | not common, hard to find |
| | *Ex.* | *This coin is very rare.* |
| **parasite** | *n.* | a living thing that lives on another living thing |
| | *Ex.* | *The flea is an example of a parasite.* |
| **vine** | *n.* | the stem of a long plant that climbs or creeps on the ground to get support |
| | *Ex.* | *The jungle has many vines.* |
| **reliance** | *n.* | dependence |
| | *Ex.* | *His reliance on his parents' aid prevents him from leaving the city.* |
| **bloom** | *v.* | to produce flowers |
| | *Ex.* | *The flowers in the garden bloom every spring.* |
| **leathery** | *adj.* | tough like leather |
| | *Ex.* | *His skin appeared thick and leathery.* |
| **petal** | *n.* | one of the often brightly colored parts of a flower that surround the reproductive organs |
| | *Ex.* | *The rose petals are red.* |
| **spike** | *n.* | thorn |
| | *Ex.* | *The plant has many spikes on its stem.* |
| **slimy** | *adj.* | covered with a sticky substance |
| | *Ex.* | *The slimy substance dripped from the ceiling.* |
| **mass** | *n.* | a body of matter usually of an indefinite shape |
| | *Ex.* | *All the items lay together in one big mass.* |
| **beneficial** | *adj.* | helpful |
| | *Ex.* | *Fruits and vegetables can be beneficial to one's health.* |

**A  Choose the best word(s) to fill in the blank.**

1. It is _____________ to see such a beautiful day during the rainy season.
   a. leathery        b. disgusting        c. sensitive        d. rare

2. The flower has such bright yellow _____________.
   a. vines        b. petals        c. masses        d. parasites

3. It is said that even the rose has _____________.
   a. vine        b. petals        c. thorns        d. shade

4. The _____________ sucks the blood of its host.
   a. parasite        b. vine        c. thorn        d. mass

5. The meat was tough and _____________.
   a. slimy        b. leathery        c. misleading        d. common

**B  Choose the correct form of the word to fill in the blanks.**

1. I am _____________ to have you as my guest.
   a. delight        b. delighted        c. delightful

2. The parasite is _____________ on its host.
   a. reliant        b. reliance        c. rely

3. When will this year's flowers _____________?
   a. bloomed        b. blooming        c. bloom

4. Vitamins can be _____________ in moderate quantities.
   a. benefactor        b. beneficially        c. beneficial

5. Sam is _____________ to my house tomorrow.
   a. came        b. come        c. coming

## Listening  T51

**Listen to the lecture and choose the best answer.**

1. What is the lecture mainly about?
   a. Flowers
   b. The pulp industry
   c. Habitats of plants
   d. Swamp Forests

2. What is true about Borneo?
   a. It is an island.
   b. It has no flowers.
   c. It is a peninsula.
   d. It's famous for its paper.

3. We can assume the lecture will continue with information about which of the following?
   a. The threat of an industry
   b. The Chilean government
   c. Education in Bornea
   d. Customs of Sumatra

## Grammar Review

**Choose the correct one.**

1. Lisa would ____________ us whenever we were in trouble.

   [and visit comfort/ visit and comfort/ and comfort visit]

2. Susie ____________ be a good doctor.

   [up grew to/ grew to up/ grew up to]

3. In ____________ to create a better world, we need to understand each other.

   [order for us/ us order for/ for us order]

4. Many patriots were ____________ for their precious country.

   [fight to ready/ to ready fight/ ready to fight]

5. The population of America is ____________ of South Korea.

   [of than that/ larger than that/ that than of]

## Vocabulary & Idioms

| | | |
|---|---|---|
| **magnificent** | *adj.* | extraordinary, fine, superb |
| | *Ex.* | *What a magnificent house!* |
| **extinct** | *adj.* | died out |
| | *Ex.* | *Dinosaurs are extinct.* |
| **habitat** | *n.* | the natural environment in which a living thing lives |
| | *Ex.* | *Turtles live in wet habitats.* |
| **ivory** | *n.* | a hard white substance from elephant tusks and walrus teeth |
| | *Ex.* | *The chopsticks are made of ivory.* |
| **tusk** | *n.* | a long, pointed, and protruding tooth |
| | *Ex.* | *Elephants have long tusks.* |
| **coat** | *n.* | the hair, fur, or wool of an animal |
| | *Ex.* | *The dog's coat is almost completely white.* |
| **endangered** | *adj.* | threatened with extinction |
| | *Ex.* | *The giant panda is endangered.* |
| **hoof** | *n.* | the foot of a horse, donkey, etc. |
| | *Ex.* | *I heard the sound of horse's hoofs.* |
| **herd** | *n.* | a group of animals that move and feed together |
| | *Ex.* | *The herd of buffalo ran past.* |
| **hide** | *n.* | the skin of a large animal |
| | *Ex.* | *Is your coat made of deer hide?* |
| **tame** | *v.* | to domesticate, to change from a wild or savage state |
| | *Ex.* | *It will take years to tame that beast.* |
| **dwindle** | *v.* | to decrease |
| | *Ex.* | *The amount of pizza left dwindled as the children ate.* |

## Vocabulary Review

**A** Choose the best word(s) to fill in the blank.

1. The horse's _____________ are injured.
   a. tusks          b. habitat          c. coats          d. hoofs

2. The rainforest is its natural _____________.
   a. habitat          b. herd          c. temple          d. laboratory

3. The dog's healthy black _____________ shined in the sunlight.
   a. tusk          b. coat          c. hoof          d. ivory

4. The piano keys are made of _____________.
   a. ivory          b. hoof          c. herd          d. habitat

5. A _____________ of elephants are drinking by the lake.
   a. habitat          b. herd          c. temple          d. laboratory

**B** Choose the correct form of the word to fill in the blanks.

1. The population is _____________.
   a. dwindled          b. dwindling          c. dwindle

2. The species is faced with _____________.
   a. extinction          b. extinct          c. extinguish

3. _____________ me at the library at 6.
   a. Met          b. Meet          c. Meeting

4. The lion _____________ has a difficult job.
   a. tamer          b. taming          c. tamed

5. The _____________ building towered over everything in the city.
   a. magnifying          b. magnificence          c. magnificent

**Listen to the lecture and choose the best answer.**

1. What is the lecture mainly about?
   a. American Bison
   b. The Plains Indians
   c. The American government
   d. Yellowstone National Park

2. What is true about the Plains Indians?
   a. They did not require bison meat and hide to live.
   b. They ate mostly bread.
   c. They were constantly at war with the American government.
   d. They are native to Canada.

3. Which is not true about the American Bison?
   a. The American Bison faced extinction at one point.
   b. Efforts to restore the American Bison have been unsuccessful.
   c. Bison are raised for meat consumption.
   d. Surviving Bison still roam Yellowstone National Park today.

**Grammar Review**

**Choose the correct one.**

1. Unfortunately, they are in ____________.
   [of disappearing danger/ of danger disappearing/ danger of disappearing]

2. They have ____________ that old house for so many years.
   [in been living/ been living in/ living been in]

3. That was ____________ furious.
   [why we got/ got we why/ why did we get]

4. She is so ____________ with.
   [talk to easy/ easy to talk/ to talk easy]

5. The horrible war ____________ 1953.
   [has been over at/ was over in/ has been over in]

## Vocabulary & Idioms

**car crash**      a serious car accident

Ex. *Fred was greatly injured in the car crash.*

**seat belt**      a belt or strap in a car that keeps a person secure

Ex. *Please wear your seatbelts.*

**fortunately**      *adv.* by good luck

Ex. *Fortunately, I was able to fix the error.*

**fatality**      *n.* a death resulting from an occurrence.

Ex. *There were over twenty fatalities in the accident.*

**dummy**      *n.* a representation of a human figure

Ex. *There were several dummies on display in the store window.*

**public**      *n.* the people of a community, state, or nation

Ex. *The musician is loved by the public.*

**feature**      *n.* a prominent or conspicuous part or characteristic

Ex. *The car has several new features.*

**sled**      *n.* a small vehicle with a platform mounted on runners

Ex. *The dogs pulled the sled as fast as they could.*

**plastic**      *adj.* made of a strong synthetic material

Ex. *Is the helmet made of plastic?*

**simulate**      *v.* to assume the appearance of

Ex. *It is hard to simulate real situations during training.*

**model**      *v.* to form or plan according to something

Ex. *The building is modeled after a similar building from a different city.*

**pregnant**      *adj.* having a child in the body.

Ex. *She's been pregnant for four months.*

## A Choose the best word(s) to fill in the blank.

1. The driver was hurt in a serious ____________.

   a. temple      b. sled      c. car crash      d. public

2. The ____________ ridiculed the President for his mistakes.

   a. features      b. public      c. car crash      d. temple

3. The ____________ toy is a favorite of the child's.

   a. endangered      b. plastic      c. pregnant      d. extinct

4. I will ____________ this character after you.

   a. tame      b. inherit      c. model      d. simulate

5. How fast can the ____________ run in snow?

   a. sled      b. herd      c. public      d. hide

## B Choose the correct form of the word to fill in the blanks.

1. Can you ____________ its appearance?

   a. simulated      b. simulating      c. simulate

2. ____________, I came prepared.

   a. Fortunate      b. Fortunately      c. Fortune

3. The accident resulted in several ____________.

   a. fatal      b. fatalities      c. fates

4. I haven't ____________ you in so long.

   a. seen      b. saw      c. see

5. The weather report says there ____________ rain tomorrow.

   a. will be      b. was      c. were

## Listening  T53

**Listen to the lecture and choose the best answer.**

1. What is the lecture mainly about?
   a. United States traffic laws
   b. Airplane pilots
   c. Drunk driving
   d. The United States military

2. What is true about drunk driving?
   a. It is safe.
   b. It is not against the law.
   c. It has caused many accidents.
   d. It only applies to car drivers.

3. Which of the following was NOT mentioned in the lecture?
   a. Drunk driving has caused over 17,000 deaths in 2003.
   b. It is illegal to drive over 70 miles per hour in some states.
   c. Airplane pilots must also follow a threshold standard.
   d. Drunk drivers can be fined.

## Grammar Review

**Choose the correct one.**

1. The programs will ______________ communication skills.
   [help improving you/ help improved your/ help improve your]

2. In fact, the building ______________ on purpose.
   [were destroying/ was destroyed/ was destroying]

3. The Williams ______________ there since 2002.
   [ lived/ live/ have been living]

4. Each ______________ an opportunity to talk with the principal.
   [students were given/ student was given/ students were giving]

5. There are ______________ disagree with the stem cell research.
   [many people who/ few people which/ a little people who]

## Vocabulary & Idioms

**suspenseful**  *adj.*  causing mental excitement or uncertainty
*Ex.  The suspenseful novel left Ted on the edge of his seat.*

**competitor**  *n.*  one who engages in a contest
*Ex.  They were both strong competitors.*

**singles**  *n.*  a tennis match with one player on each side
*Ex.  Have you ever played in a singles match?*

**round**  *n.*  one of a series of courses in some play or sport
*Ex.  How many rounds are left?*

**opponent**  *n.*  a person on the opposing side of a game, contest, or conflict
*Ex.  My opponent was much more experienced than me.*

**media**  *n.*  a means of communication such as by newspaper, TV, radio, etc.
*Ex.  Many important events are reported by the media.*

**stardom**  *n.*  great fame of a singer, actor, musician, etc.
*Ex.  He quickly rose to stardom for his talents.*

**rank**  *n.*  to assign to a particular position, class, etc.
*Ex.  Max was ranked fifth out of twenty athletes.*

**professional**  *adj.*  following an occupation as a means of livelihood
*Ex.  Michael Jordan was a professional basketball player.*

**elite**  *n.*  the best of anything that is considered collectively as a group, class, etc.
*Ex.  Only the elite can survive here.*

**coach**  *n.*  a person who trains athletes
*Ex.  Who is your football coach?*

**pro**  *adj.*  short for professional
*Ex.  Pro athletes train very hard every day.*

## Vocabulary Review

**A  Choose the best word(s) to fill in the blank.**

1. Is this a ______________ or doubles match?
   a. media          b. opponent          c. triples          d. singles

2. He began to get tired during the second ______________.
   a. rank          b. round          c. competitor          d. opponent

3. The ______________ barked out commands to the team.
   a. elite          b. coach          c. media          d. public

4. It may take years of hard work before he can reach ______________.
   a. stardom          b. the elite          c. an opponent          d. a competitor

5. Fred tried his hardest to beat his ______________.
   a. proponent          b. competitor          c. sled          d. herd

**B  Choose the correct form of the word to fill in the blanks.**

1. We need a ______________ coach to teach us how to play the sport.
   a. profession          b. professional          c. professionally

2. The car that I ______________ to you is still in top condition.
   a. gave          b. give          c. given

3. The fastest ______________ won the match.
   a. competition          b. competitor          c. compete

4. An ______________ warrior fights to the last breath.
   a. elite          b. elitist          c. elitism

5. I can't sand the ______________!
   a. suspense          b. suspenseful          c. suspend

**Listen to the lecture and choose the best answer.**

1. What is the lecture mainly about?
   a. Major Walter Clopton Wingfield's life
   b. French sports
   c. Spanish sports
   d. The creation of tennis

2. What is true about Major Walter Clopton Wingfield?
   a. He patented the game of tennis.　　b. He created the game in France.
   c. He also created basketball.　　d. He is still alive.

3. What French word does the word "tennis" come from?
   a. tenir　　　　　　　　　　b. tenez
   c. teneur　　　　　　　　　d. trillion


## Grammar Review

**Choose the correct one.**

1. Many ____________ during that period.
   [discoveries was made/ discoveries were made/ discovery was made]

2. Unfortunately, our soldiers ____________ the battle.
   [began lose/ lost beginning/ began losing]

3. Lots of people ____________ the beauty of the temple.
   [were amazed by/ was amazing by/ were amazing by]

4. ____________ were in class.
   [Almost students/ Almost student/ Most students]

5. Fortunately, they are ____________ now.
   [feeling much better/ felt more better/ feeling very better]

## Vocabulary & Idioms

**destructive** — *adj.* tending to destroy
*Ex.* *The destructive fire ruined many homes.*

**earthquake** — *n.* a shaking of the earth's crust
*Ex.* *An earthquake occurred last night.*

**regulation** — *n.* a rule
*Ex.* *The regulations state that you must take off your shoes before you enter the building.*

**vulnerable** — *adj.* open to assault, difficult to defend
*Ex.* *Without armor, the warrior was vulnerable.*

**engineer** — *n.* a person trained in the design of machines
*Ex.* *The company is now hiring electrical engineers.*

**nickname** — *v.* to give a name to be used instead of the real or proper name
*Ex.* *My nickname in school was Chuckles because I was always laughing.*

**weight** — *n.* any heavy load, mass, or object
*Ex.* *Lifting weights is a good way to exercise.*

**stabilize** — *v.* to maintain an unchanging level or quantity
*Ex.* *You must learn to stabilize your temper.*

**brace** — *n.* something that holds parts together or in a place
*Ex.* *After dislocating your arm, you need a brace to keep it in place for a few months.*

**jet** — *n.* a stream of liquid, gas, or small solid particles
*Ex.* *Jets of water shot forth from the bursting pipe.*

**program** — *v.* to insert specific instructions into a machine
*Ex.* *Elliot programmed the device to detect intruders.*

**react** — *v.* to act in response to something
*Ex.* *Angie reacted by screaming at the top of her lungs.*

## A Choose the best word(s) to fill in the blank.

1. The ______________ is holding everything in place.
   a. brace　　　　b. jet　　　　c. regulation　　　　d. engineer

2. Can you ______________ the machine to start running at 7pm?
   a. nickname　　　　b. program　　　　c. stabilize　　　　d. rank

3. He's at the gym lifting ______________.
   a. weights　　　　b. braces　　　　c. media　　　　d. dummies

4. He is a ______________ athlete.
   a. vulnerable　　　　b. pro　　　　c. suspenseful　　　　d. plastic

5. I ______________ him the Bomb.
   a. stabilized　　　　b. reacted　　　　c. ranked　　　　d. nicknamed

## B Choose the correct form of the word to fill in the blanks.

1. The earthquake was so ______________ that it wiped out half the city.
   a. destructive　　　　b. destruction　　　　c. destroy

2. Is there a way we can ______________ the numbers?
   a. stable　　　　b. stability　　　　c. stabilize

3. Sam's ______________ was very sad.
   a. react　　　　b. reaction　　　　c. reacting

4. Right now I am very ______________ to insults.
   a. vulnerability　　　　b. vulnerable　　　　c. vulnerably

5. What do the ______________ say?
   a. regulation　　　　b. regulations　　　　c. regulate

## Listening  T55

**Listen to the lecture and choose the best answer.**

1. What is the lecture mainly about?
   a. Alaska
   b. The Pacific Ocean
   c. The occurrence of earthquakes
   d. The Pacific Ring of Fire

2. Where are earthquakes most likely to occur?
   a. Alaska
   b. The Pacific Ocean
   c. The Atlantic Ocean
   d. The Pacific Ring of Fire

3. What do scientists use to report earthquakes?
   a. Satellites
   b. Seismic stations
   c. Submarines
   d. Weather balloons

## Grammar Review

**Choose the correct one.**

1. Albert Einstein was one of ______________ in the 20th century.
   [a greatest scientist / the greatest scientists / the great scientist]

2. It was in 1999 ______________ Paris for the first time.
   [where they visiting / when they visited / that they visited]

3. Cindy ______________ many countries since she was a child.
   [traveling to / has traveled to / traveled to]

4. The pictures on the wall ______________ at night.
   [look pretty scary / look pretty scarily / looking pretty scared]

5. Try to ______________ so that you can master the skill.
   [kept practice / kept practiced / keep practicing]

# Let's Garden for a Healthier Life!



**serene**    *adj.*   calm

     *Ex.*   *They sat on the porch enjoying the cool, serene evening.*

**trim**    *v.*   to cut down

     *Ex.*   *Please trim the bushes.*

**fresh**    *adj.*   looking youthful and helpful, newly arrived

     *Ex.*   *The farmer harvested the fresh fruit.*

**weed**    *v.*   to remove weeds or valueless and troublesome plant that grows where it is not wanted

     *Ex.*   *After weeding the garden, Sarah continued to water her flowers.*

**scent**    *n.*   a usually agreeable smell

     *Ex.*   *The roses have a nice scent.*

**various**    *adj.*   of different kinds

     *Ex.*   *The box contains various kinds of chocolates.*

**soil**    *n.*   the ground as producing vegetation or as cultivated for its crops

     *Ex.*   *The land is rich in soil for crops.*

**sense**    *n.*   feeling

     *Ex.*   *The meeting left me with a sense of awkwardness.*

**result**    *n.*   something that happens as a consequence, outcome

     *Ex.*   *The results of the examination did not turn out good.*

**ill**    *adj.*   sick

     *Ex.*   *He became ill from drinking too much beer.*

**patient**    *n.*   a person who is being treated medically

     *Ex.*   *I'm visiting a patient at the St. James Hospital.*

**basically**    *adv.*   for the most part

     *Ex.*   *I basically do whatever I want to on weekends.*

## Vocabulary Review

**A  Choose the best word(s) to fill in the blank.**

1. Can you please ____________ my hair a bit?
   a. weed          b. trim          c. stabilize          d. rank

2. The night sky appeared calm and ____________.
   a. various          b. high          c. serene          d. lazy

3. He's been ____________ with a virus for a few days now.
   a. fresh          b. ill          c. lazy          d. sleepy

4. ____________, I go to the gym whenever I have time.
   a. Eventually          b. Basically          c. Especially          d. Occasionally

5. The ____________ sat waiting to be treated by the doctor.
   a. patients          b. champions          c. lizards          d. professors

**B  Choose the correct form of the word to fill in the blanks.**

1. Do you want ____________ to the pool?
   a. go          b. went          c. to go

2. How many more hours will it ____________?
   a. take          b. took          c. taken

3. The ____________ colored lights on the Christmas tree shown brightly.
   a. variation          b. various          c. variable

4. The ____________ made cookies were delicious.
   a. freshly          b. fresh          c. freshness

5. I hope I am not ____________ you.
   a. bother          b. bothering          c. bothered

### Listen to the lecture and choose the best answer.

1. What is the lecture mainly about?
   a. Types of stress
   b. Economic conditions
   c. Strength training
   d. Gardening

2. Which type of stress improves function?
   a. Distress
   b. Eustress
   c. Mistress
   d. Work stress

3. What is true about distress?
   a. Distress can result from having enough sleep.
   b. Distress occurs when personal expectations and reality are the same.
   c. Distress results from unresolved stress and can cause anxiety or illness.
   d. Distress is not a serious problem.

## Grammar Review

### Choose the correct one.

1. Approximately 35% of ____________ single parents.
   [the student has / student have / the students have]

2. The ____________ about the mermaid engaged the entire audience.
   [fascinated story / fascinating story / fascinated stories]

3. Many students spend most of ____________ computer games.
   [their time to play / his time playing / their time playing]

4. Some of the TV programs make the ____________ about themselves.
   [viewer felt badly / viewers feel bad / viewers feel badly]

5. ____________ up requires a sense of responsibility.
   [Growing / Grow up / Grown]

## Vocabulary & Idioms

**rumor**    *n.*    a circulating story that has not been confirmed to be true
       *Ex.*   *There is a rumor that a witch lives in the house down the street.*

**monster**    *n.*    an animal or thing huge in size and frightening
       *Ex.*   *Many stories involve monsters.*

**ancient**    *adj.*    of a very long time ago
       *Ex.*   *Ancient cities have risen and fallen.*

**spot**    *v.*    to see
       *Ex.*   *I spotted a tall building in the distance.*

**dinosaur**    *n.*    a giant prehistoric lizard that no longer exists
       *Ex.*   *Dinosaurs once roamed the earth.*

**photograph**    *n.*    a picture recorded by a camera
       *Ex.*   *This is a photograph of my dog Pup.*

**investigate**    *v.*    to examine, study, or inquire into systematically
       *Ex.*   *The police investigated the mystery.*

**radar**    *n.*    a device for determining an object's presence by using radio waves
       *Ex.*   *Two unidentified objects are showing on the radar.*

**sound wave**    a longitudinal pressure wave of audible sound
       *Ex.*   *The machine measures sound waves.*

**weird**    *adj.*    strange
       *Ex.*   *The dessert has a weird taste.*

**monitor**    *n.*    a receiver, such as a screen or speaker, that is used to check the quality or content of an electronic transmission
       *Ex.*   *What does it say on the monitor?*

**myth**    *n.*    an imaginary, fictitious thing
       *Ex.*   *Many children believe in the myth of Santa Clause.*

**A  Choose the best word(s) to fill in the blank.**

1. Did you hear the ___________ about Sam's injury?
   a. monster          b. rumor          c. myth          d photograph

2. This is a lovely ___________ of you and your family.
   a. photograph     b. rumor          c. myth          d. monster

3. ___________ have been extinct for a very long time.
   a. monsters        b. dinosaurs     c. myths         d. rumors

4. We need to ___________ this problem further.
   a. spot               b. use             c. investigate   d. list

5. The movie is too ___________ for my taste.
   a. weird             b. ill              c. rude           d. quiet

**B  Choose the correct form of the word to fill in the blanks.**

1. I'm waiting ___________ the movie next week.
   a. to see                    b. saw                    c. seeing

2. The plane ___________ in a few more hours.
   a. will arrive              b. arrived               c. arriving

3. The dragon is a ___________ creature.
   a. myth                     b. mythically          c. mythical

4. I can't ___________ for the new CD to arrive in stores.
   a. wait                      b. waited               c. will wait

5. There are several ways ___________ the problem.
   a. solve                     b. to solve             c. solved

## Listening  T57

**Listen to the lecture and choose the best answer.**

1. What is the lecture mainly about?

   a. Bertram Mills' circus

   b. Possible explanations for Nessie sightings

   c. Elephants and their bathing habits

   d. Eels and dolphins.

2. Which of the following was NOT a suggestion mentioned in the lecture?

   a. Nessie is a large sea turtle.          b. Nessie is a circus elephant.

   c. Nessie is an eel.                       d. Nessie is a dolphin.

3. What is Nessie supposed to be?

   a. A three-eyed frog                       b. A kangaroo

   c. A circus elephant                       d. A monster

## Grammar Review

**Choose the correct one.**

1. That is the ______________ I have ever seen.

   [more beautiful scene/ much beautiful scenes/ most beautiful scene]

2. They heard Nancy ______________ the piano so beautifully.

   [to play/ play/ played]

3. The images were ______________ everyone was astounded.

   [such shocking when/ so shocked when/ so shocking that]

4. We had great difficulty ______________ told us.

   [understood what he/ understanding what he/ to understand that he]

5. Finally, the school ______________ more money in the poor students.

   [decided to invest/ decided investing/ decide investing]

## Vocabulary & Idioms

**atmosphere**    *n.*    the gaseous envelope that surrounds the Earth
*Ex.*   *The atmosphere is made up of many different gases.*

**ultraviolet rays**    rays of light that produce wavelengths beyond the violet of the spectrum
*Ex.*   *Ultraviolet rays are harmful to the skin.*

**layer**    *n.*    a horizontal expanse
*Ex.*   *The cake has four layers.*

**cancer**    *n.*    a disease resulting from the abnormal growth of cells
*Ex.*   *The old lady was being treated for cancer.*

**shock**    *n.*    something that jars the mind or emotions
*Ex.*   *The situation left him in shock.*

**future**    *n.*    time that is to come after
*Ex.*   *It is time to plan for the future.*

**refrigerator**    *n.*    a box in which food is kept cool
*Ex.*   *What's left in the refrigerator?*

**air conditioner**    a device used to lower the temperature of a room
*Ex.*   *It's nice to be in a room with an air conditioner on a very hot day.*

**insect**    *n.*    very small animals with bodies divided into three parts
*Ex.*   *Be careful of insects.*

**damage**    *n.*    injury or harm that reduces usefulness
*Ex.*   *The storm caused much damage to the house.*

**replace**    *v.*    to take the place of something
*Ex.*   *Can you replace this broken one with a new one?*

**repair**    *v.*    to fix
*Ex.*   *Steve went to the get his car repaired.*

## Vocabulary Review

**A  Choose the best word(s) to fill in the blank.**

1. Should we add another ____________ of paint?
   a. atmosphere      b. air conditioner      c. layer      d. refrigerator

2. Please throw out the old food in the ____________.
   a. atmosphere      b. air conditioner      c. layer      d. refrigerator

3. Can you turn up the ____________?
   a. atmosphere      b. air conditioner      c. layer      d. future

4. No one knows what's in store for the ____________.
   a. atmosphere      b. air conditioner      c. layer      d. future

5. We must protect the ozone layer in the Earth's ____________.
   a. atmosphere      b. air conditioner      c. layer      d. future

**B  Choose the correct form of the word to fill in the blanks.**

1. I need someone ____________ the TV.
   a. repair                b. to repair                c. repairing

2. The old furniture ____________ yesterday.
   a. replaced              b. replacement              c. was replaced

3. They were ready to ____________ their country from the enemy.
   a. protect               b. protection               c. protective

4. The category ____________ many different subcategories.
   a. inclusive             b. includes                 c. inclusion

5. Do we have any meat ____________?
   a. left                  b. leave                    c. will leave

**Listen to the lecture and choose the best answer.**

1. What is the lecture mainly about?
   a. Firefighting techniques
   b. Hospital hygiene standards
   c. More uses of ozone
   d. Water treatment

2. Which substance does ozone replace in many water treatment facilities?
   a. Hydrogen
   b. Steel
   c. Chlorine
   d. Salt

3. How is ozone used in the situation of a fire?
   a. Firefighters use ozone to clean the air.
   b. Ozone, when mixed with water, helps put out fires more quickly.
   c. Firefighters use ozone to clean the uniforms.
   d. Ozone mixed with gasoline can make fire trucks run faster.

**Grammar Review**

**Choose the correct one.**

1. Many species, ____________ whales and dolphins, breathe through lungs.
   [include/ including/ included]

2. A totally new building ____________ on the site.
   [is been built/ is being build/ is being built]

3. A variety of fertilizers ____________ help plants to grow well.
   [are used to/ are using/ use to]

4. ____________ rich, Maria did not feel happy.
   [Despite she was/ Although her/ Although she was]

5. To lead a better life, you should ____________ .
   [stop making excuses/ stop to make excuses/ stopped making excuses]

# 19   Giant Otters

## Vocabulary & Idioms

**timid**    *adj.*   meek, shy
*Ex.*   *He's always been a timid boy in class.*

**sleek**    *adj.*   trim and graceful
*Ex.*   *My new sports car has a sleek body.*

**cousin**    *n.*   a member of a kindred group or country
*Ex.*   *Our primate cousins are less intelligent but much stronger and more agile.*

**jaguar**    *n.*   a large, spotted feline that lives in tropical regions
*Ex.*   *Have you ever come across a ferocious jaguar before?*

**slash**    *v.*   to cut with a violent sweep
*Ex.*   *The warrior slashed with his sword.*

**belly**    *n.*   the stomach
*Ex.*   *My belly hurts from eating too much.*

**diet**    *n.*   a particular selection of food
*Ex.*   *The rabbit lives on a diet of fruits or vegetables.*

**herd**    *v.*   to lead or drive a group to a destination
*Ex.*   *The farmer herded the cattle into the truck.*

**benefit**    *n.*   something that is advantageous or good
*Ex.*   *Are there any benefits of working at your new job?*

**participate**    *v.*   to join in
*Ex.*   *I would like to participate in the soccer game.*

**cub**    *n.*   the young of certain animals such as the bear, lion, otter, etc.
*Ex.*   *Lion cubs are quite large at birth.*

**technique**    *n.*   way of doing or accomplishing something
*Ex.*   *Teach me the best business techniques.*

**A Choose the best word(s) to fill in the blank.**

1. Frank _____________ the door open with a knife.
   a. repaired     b. slashed     c. kicked     d. punched

2. I am going on a _____________ of only eating vegetables.
   a. benefit     b. diet     c. cruise     d. ride

3. The cat purred as I rubbed its _____________ .
   a. eyes     b. food     c. bed     d. belly

4. Tell me what my _____________ are of coming to live here.
   a. benefits     b. characteristics     c. dreams     d. thoughts

5. Don't be so _____________ when meeting new people.
   a. smart     b. handsome     c. timid     d. rusty

**B Choose the correct form of the word to fill in the blanks.**

1. Mom _____________ us out the door and into the car.
   a. herd     b. herding     c. herded

2. Did you _____________ in sports in high school?
   a. participated     b. participating     c. participate

3. Don't ignore _____________ people!
   a. ugly     b. ugliness     c. uglily

4. We need to _____________ its strength.
   a. measurement     b. measure     c. measurer

5. I sometimes _____________ pink with violet.
   a. confusion     b. confusedly     c. confuse

## Listening  T59

**Listen to the lecture and choose the best answer.**

1. What is the lecture mainly about?
   a. Animal hunting methods
   b. Other animals that live in groups
   c. Lions
   d. Fish habitats

2. What are the groups in which fish live together called?
   a. Prides
   b. Herds
   c. Triads
   d. Schools

3. What is a benefit of being in a school?
   a. Better chances of mating
   b. Warmer environment
   c. Cooler environments
   d. More space to swim

## Grammar Review

**Choose the correct one.**

1. Did you know that _____________ righteous people out there?
   [there is many / are there many / there are many]

2. The restaurant was _____________ than we had expected.
   [very more expensive / much more expensive / very expensive]

3. While _____________, Anna went to many old buildings.
   [visiting the country / visited the country / visit a country]

4. All the students _____________ the event a success.
   [participated in to make / participates in made / participated in making]

5. When _____________, let me know immediately.
   [arrived / they arrive / they will arrive]

# 20 The Cliff Dwellers



**cave** — *n.* a horizontal hollow area in a mountain or a hill.
*Ex.* *The bear lives in a cave.*

**empire** — *n.* a group of nations or peoples ruled by an emperor, empress, or some other powerful sovereign or government
*Ex.* *The Roman Empire encompassed almost all of Europe at one point in history.*

**ruins** — *n.* the remains of a building, city, etc. that has been destroyed
*Ex.* *These are the ruins left behind from the earthquake.*

**decay** — *v.* to rot, to become decomposed
*Ex.* *The leftover food is starting to decay.*

**cliff** — *n.* a high steep face of a rock
*Ex.* *The cliff was so high that it was hard to see the top.*

**go back in time** — to go to the past
*Ex.* *He wished he could make a time machine that would allow him to go back in time.*

**squash** — *n.* the fruit of a vine-like plant, usually eaten as a vegetable
*Ex.* *The pilgrims ate turkey and squash for Thanksgiving.*

**plentiful** — *adj.* many, abundant
*Ex.* *The tree has plentiful flowers.*

**raid** — *v.* to make a surprise attack
*Ex.* *The enemy soldiers raided the homes of the civilians.*

**survival** — *n.* the act of remaining alive or in existence
*Ex.* *The survival of the Plains Indians depended on buffalo meat for food.*

**dwelling** — *n.* home
*Ex.* *We have a humble dwelling in Florida where we like to go in the winter.*

## Vocabulary Review

**A Choose the best word(s) to fill in the blank.**

1. The corpse ____________ after a few months.
   a. decayed          b. cried          c. flew          d. grew

2. I wish I could ____________ to correct my mistakes.
   a. grow tall        b. go back in time  c. run faster    d. eat well

3. Be careful not to stand at the edge of the ____________ or you may fall.
   a. ruins            b. cliff          c. empire        d. cave

4. I'm going to the supermarket to buy some beef and ____________ for dinner.
   a. glue             b. squash         c. pencils       d. detergent

5. Archaeologists are searching the ____________ of the ancient city.
   a. ruins            b. empire         c. kings         d. food

**B Choose the correct form of the word to fill in the blanks.**

1. There is ____________ of rice in the pantry.
   a. plentiful            b. plentifully            c. plenty

2. We ____________ the enemy base in seven hours.
   a. raiding             b. will raid              c. raider

3. Can we continue ____________?
   a. to win             b. won                    c. will win

4. We cannot guarantee the ____________ of everyone.
   a. survive            b. survival               c. survived

5. Sadly, the city was ____________ by a fire.
   a. destructive        b. destroyed              c. destruction

**Listen to the lecture and choose the best answer.**

1. What is the lecture mainly about?
   a. Mexican customs
   b. The Pueblo Indians
   c. More information about cliff dwellings
   d. American history

2. Which of the following places was NOT mentioned in the lecture?
   a. Mexico
   b. New Mexico
   c. Texas
   d. Colorado

3. What is true about the cliff dwellings?
   a. Cliff dwellings are very unsafe.
   b. Some Native Americans still use cliff dwellings today.
   c. The age of the cliff dwellings has been confirmed.
   d. There are three types of cliff dwellings.

## Grammar Review

**Choose the correct one.**

1. Unfortunately, there _____________ people who try to achieve their goals by using unethical methods.
   [is so many / are so many / are any]

2. _____________ were against the new legislation.
   [million of worker / million of workers / millions of workers]

3. _____________, you can definitely improve your reading skills.
   [By reading extensively / By to read extensive / In reading extensive]

4. They were impressed by the _____________ building.
   [ten-stories / ten-story / ten-floors]

5. _____________ foreign language is a long, hard process.
   [Mastering a / Master the / Mastered a]

# BuildUp Reading Level 1
## Workbook